박문각의 합격 노하우와
편입에 특화된 커리큘럼

편입의 마스터키
박문각 편입 영어

실전 독해

Reading

홍준기 편저

합격기준 박문각 편입

PMG 박문각

머리말
PREFACE

저자가 오랜 기간 편입 독해 영역을 강의하면서 느낀 점은 시험의 수준이 점점 높아지고 있다는 것이다. 지문은 점점 어려워지고 문제는 점점 세련되어진다. 적당히 감으로 풀 수 있는 수준은 지난 지 오래고, 해외에서 6~8년 이상의 정규 과정을 마치고 귀국한 학생들이 편입 시험의 대열에 합류하면서 더욱더 난이도가 높아지고 있다. 그렇지만 편입 시험도 평가 시험이므로 가장 최적화된 방법으로 효율적으로 열심히 공부하면 분명히 결실을 맺을 수 있다. 그럼에도 불구하고 아직도 잘못된 독해 학습법으로 수험생들의 아까운 시간을 허비하는 경우가 많아서 안타까울 따름이다. 불확실한 현대 사회에서 자기 판단을 신뢰하지 못하는 경우가 많다 보니, 수험생들도 주변의 얘기에 휘둘리며 자신만의 체계적인 독해 학습을 하지 못하는 경우가 허다하다. 독해의 올바른 정도는 많이 읽고 많이 생각하는 것으로, 체계적으로 글을 읽으면서 이해하는 법을 터득하면 된다. 체계적으로 학습하면 그리 오래 걸리는 과정이 아닌데도, 학생들은 성급한 마음에 정도를 걷지 못하고 샛길로 빠져든다. 그러다 1년이라는 시간이 거의 지날 무렵 문제점을 파악하는 경우가 종종 있다. 이런 사태를 미연에 방지하기 위해서는 처음부터 체계적인 방향성을 정립한 후 자신만의 로드맵을 작성하여 시험에 임해야만 오류를 줄일 수 있다.

이 책의 특징에 대해서 간단히 언급하자면,

첫째, 본서의 20회 자료는 저자 본인이 직접 읽고 편입에 적합하게 일부를 변형한 후 문제를 하나하나 현재의 편입 시험 경향에 맞추어 만들었다. 학생들이 풀면서 난이도가 너무 높거나 혼동을 초래할 만한 문제는 피드백을 통하여 제외하고 원어민 교수의 감수를 통하여 영문에 대한 교열을 하였다. 그러므로 수록된 문장 하나하나가 다 정확하고 오류가 없는 글이므로 문제풀이 연습뿐 아니라 학생들의 읽기 능력 향상에도 도움을 줄 것이다.

둘째, 수록된 지문으로 고전과 시사적인 글을 망라하였으며, 추상적인 글과 구체적인 글들을 균형감 있게 수록하였다. 철학, 논리학, 자연과학 그리고 인터넷에 이르기까지 다양한 글들을 읽고 푸는 과정을 통해 여러 저자의 문체에 익숙해지고 글의 다양한 구성을 이해할 수 있을 것이다. 다만 시중의 그 어떤 교재보다도 지문의 난이도가 높아서 학습에 어려움이 있을 수 있다. 그러므로 체계적으로 학습을 꾸준히 해야 하며, 그렇게 20회분을 풀고 나면 독해에 대해 자신감이 생길 것이다.

셋째, 본서의 20회분 문제는 난이도를 높이기 위하여 까다롭지만 근거가 명확한 문제를 만들어서 수록하였다. 최근의 시험 경향이 단순히 'fit'을 고르는 게 아닌 'best fit'을 고르는 식으로 전환되어 더욱 까다로워졌으므로 이에 적합한 훈련을 하고자 하였다. 지문만 이해하면 답이 저절로 나오는 문제가 아닌, 고민하고 풀 수 있는 문제들을 수록하였다. 더불어 paraphrase 문제와 추론 문제 등 타 교재에서는 접하기 쉽지 않은 문제들도 다수 수록하였다.

넷째, 모든 지문의 해설에 만전을 기하였으며, 문제의 보기 하나하나 모두 해석을 달았다. 지문을 읽고도 문제의 보기를 이해하지 못해 틀리는 경우가 있으므로 이를 방지하는 차원에서 그리고 독학하는 학생들에게 강의 없이도 이해할 수 있도록 하기 위하여 철저한 해설을 달았으며, 어휘도 자세히 수록하였다. 지문을 읽고 복습하는 과정에서 상당한 시간을 절약할 수 있을 것이다. 오답의 근거를 제시하지 않는 여타 교재와는 다르게 일일이 선택지를 해석하였으므로 이를 바탕으로 자신이 스스로 오답의 근거를 찾을 수 있도록 배려하였다.

〈박문각 편입 실전 독해〉를 집필하는 데 도움을 준 모든 분들에게 감사의 인사를 전한다. 먼저 이 책의 초안이 되는 모의고사 강평 강의에 참여해서 수준 높은 질의응답으로 저자로 하여금 책의 해설을 자세히 달 수 있도록 해 준 수강생들, 이 책을 믿고 공부하여 원하는 대학에 진학을 했던 사랑하는 제자들, 그리고 이 책의 완성도를 위해 힘써 준 출판사의 관계자 여러분께도 감사의 마음을 전한다.
마지막으로 이 책으로 공부하게 될 수험생들에게 힘들겠지만 노력하는 자에게만 미래가 있다는 사실을 언제나 잊지 말기를 바란다. 나보다 앞선 자를 바라보며 성실하고 겸손하게 하루하루 임한다면 결국 이룰 수 있다는, 공부하는 자들의 진리를 전하고 싶다.

2021년 7월

저자 홍준기

이 책의 활용 방법
GUIDE

1단계

이 책은 마무리 교재로 기획한 것으로, 초급용으로는 적당하지 않고 적어도 중상급 이상의 수험생이라야 도움이 된다. 아직 수준에 오르지 않았다면 조금 더 독해력을 다진 뒤에 이 책으로 돌아오길 권한다. 적어도 여름이 지나면서 학습하길 바란다. 기존에 나온 어떤 독해 서적보다도 실전에 가까운 난이도 있는 교재이므로 어렵다는 것을 미리 알고 풀기 바란다.

2단계

이 책은 최적화된 난이도를 바탕으로 시간 대비 훈련이 핵심이다. 30분 안에 20문제, 45분 안에 30문제를 풀어야 하므로 시간이 부족할 수밖에 없다. 이런 시간 적응 훈련은 매우 중요한데, 실제 이렇게 훈련을 했던 학생들은 시험장에서 시간이 부족한 곤란을 겪지 않았다. 45분 안에 쉽지 않은 지문 10개를, 그것도 쉽지 않은 난도의 30문제를 푸는 것은 너무 고된 일이다. 하지만 이런 과정을 거치면 독해력에 대한 실력이 향상되고 자신감이 배양될 것이다. 처음부터 시간에 얽매이는 것이 부담스러운 경우에는 몇 회씩 나눠서 시간을 조금씩 단축해 가는 것도 한 방법이다. 처음에는 시간보다 5~10분 더 잡고 풀고, 나중에는 제 시간에 맞추면 된다. 하지만 이 경우 합격생들과의 비교는 무리가 있으므로 자신이 효과적으로 순서를 정해서 학습하길 바란다.

3단계

한 회씩 풀고 피드백을 철저히 해야 한다. 어려운 글들이 많으므로 한 번 읽고 지나가지 말고 합격생들의 조언처럼 철저히 자기화하는 과정을 거쳐야 한다. 다양한 글들을 수록했기 때문에 자신에게 취약한 분야도 있을 것이고, 해석과 해설을 봐도 쉽게 이해하지 못하는 글들도 있을 것이다. 그럴 때는 백과사전이나 관련 기사의 글들을 검색해서 읽어 보는 것도 도움이 된다. 하지만 유념해야 될 것은 언제나 우리는 독해 시험을 준비하는 것이지 상식 시험을 보는 것이 아니므로 배경지식에 너무 집착할 필요는 없다는 점이다. 지문 안에서 근거를 찾아서 푸는 것이 정석이며, 이런 훈련을 통해 글 읽기가 정교해지는 것이다.

본문에 나오는 어휘들을 철저히 숙지해야 한다. 어휘는 글을 통하여 익히는 것이 최선의 방법이지만, 그렇게 많은 글을 읽을 수 없기 때문에 궁여지책으로 어휘집을 보는 것이다. 그런데 오히려 학생들은 주객이 전도되어 어휘집에서 본 어휘가 독해에 나오면 반가워한다. 이는 바람직한 학습이 아니며 독해에서 나온 어휘를 먼저 숙지하고 독해에 빈출되지 않지만 어휘 시험에 자주 나오는 어휘를 따로 학습해야 하는 것이다. 참고로 어휘의 단권화 작업이 아직 되지 않은 수험생들은 저자가 쓴 〈박문각 편입 실전 어휘〉의 어휘 학습법을 참조하여 방향성을 정립하기 바란다. 문법과 어휘는 결국 독해를 잘하기 위한 도구라는 점을 명심해야 한다.

5단계

학생들이 독해 문제를 푸는 데 걸리는 시간을 정확히 판단하지 못하기 때문에 독해만의 시간 훈련이 중요하다. 교재에서 10회까지는 20문제로, 11회부터 20회까지는 30문제로 구성한 것은 각 학교별로 문제의 개수가 다르기 때문이다. 가능하면 각 회에 맞추어 시간 연습을 하길 바란다. 하지만 마무리 단계에서는 전체 영역이 수록된 모의고사를 시간에 맞춰 풀어보길 바란다. 곧 출간될 예정(2021.9.)인 〈박문각 편입 적중모의고사〉가 이에 최적화된 교재이므로, 이를 통해 실전 대비 훈련을 하면 동반 상승의 효과가 있을 것이다.

선배의 학습법
GUIDE

“

이 휘 (2020년 박문각 편입 수강생, 서강대 경제학과 일반편입 합격)

들어가며

저는 2020년 박문각편입학원에서 공부했고, 서강대 경제학과에 합격한 학생입니다. 저 또한 이 책을 보고 공부를 한 입장에서 이 책을 효율적으로 활용하는 방법에 대해 저의 경험을 바탕으로 적도록 하겠습니다. 〈박문각 편입 실전 독해〉에 나온 지문과 문제는 난도가 높은 편이지만, 독해 실력을 테스트하기에 좋은 구성이므로 어느 정도의 실력이 쌓인 후 학습하면 훨씬 도움이 될 것입니다.

독해 영역의 중요성

대부분의 편입영어 시험은 60분의 시험 시간동안 40문제를 푸는 구성이며, 첫 20여 분 동안 어휘, 문법, 논리 영역을 모두 푼 뒤 나머지 40분간 집중력을 유지하며 독해 영역을 해결해야 하는 시험입니다. 다시 말해, 독해 영역이야말로 편입영어 시험의 변별력과 당락을 가르는 중추적인 영역이라고 할 수 있겠습니다. 또한 학교에 따라 독해 문제에 추가 배점을 가하는 경우가 더러 있으며, 추가 배점이 없다 하더라도 앞서 말한 변별력을 시험하는 부분이기에 그 중요성은 아무리 강조해도 지나치지 않을 것입니다.

독해력 및 문제해결능력 배양

모든 정신적 능력은 물리적인 근육처럼 계속해서 사용해야 그 능력이 길러집니다. 본 책은 그 점을 고려하여, 독해력과 문제해결능력을 배양할 수 있도록 풍부하게 구성되어 있습니다. 20세트로 구성된 본 책은 단문부터 장문까지 다양한 형태의 지문들을 각종 문헌에서 발췌하여 풍부하게 수록하고 있습니다. 이 지문들은 글의 형식, 문제의 형식, 주제의 다양성, 문장의 해석 난이도 등 많은 요소들을 고려하여 엄선된 지문들로, 본 책에 수록된 지문을 빼놓지 않고 제대로 독해하는 경험 자체로도 독해력 배양에 큰 도움이 되었습니다. 또한, 다양하고 수준 높은 문제들을 경험하면서 문제해결능력도 길렀습니다. 여러분들도 저처럼 이 책에 수록된 지문과 문제를 빠짐없이 소화한다는 각오로 임하시기 바랍니다.

시간관리와 실전감각

독해 시험에 임할 때는 40여 분의 시간 동안 20~30문제를 풀며 집중력을 잃지 않는 것, 그리고 필요할 때 과감한 결정을 내려 흐름을 잃지 않는 것이 중요합니다. 20~30문제씩 묶여 있는 책의 구성은 그런 흐름을 몸에 익히는 데 큰 도움을 줍니다. Practice Set당 배정된 시간을 꼭 지켜 문제를 풀고 시간 관리에 대한 감을 익히시기 바랍니다. 또한 문제를 풀며 체감상 어느 정도의 시간을 써야 하는지, 또 유력한 오답과 정답 사이에서 고민이 될 때 어떻게 과감하게 결단을 내리고 다음 문제로 넘어가야 하는지 등, 실전에서 당락을 좌우할 수 있는 결정들을 미리 해 봄으로써 실전과 유사한 경험들을 쌓아야 합니다. 이러한 경험이 풍부해질수록 본인이 순간순간 내리는 결정에 자신감을 가질 수 있게 되며, 전체적인 수험의 흐름에도 긍정적으로 작용하게 될 것입니다. 문제를 풀고 채점하는 데서 그치지 마시고, 왜 맞는지, 왜 틀리는지에 대해 짧게 메모하는 식으로라도 정리하는 습관을 들이시기 바랍니다.

배경지식

본 책에 수록된 지문들의 내용을 제대로 이해하고 정리하는 경험을 쌓다 보면, 지문과 관련된 배경지식들이 자연스럽게 쌓이게 될 것입니다. 단순히 문제를 푸는 것뿐 아니라, 스스로 지문을 제대로 해석해 보고 정리하는 경험을 쌓다 보면 배경지식이 쌓이게 됩니다. 편입 독해에는 출제 범위가 없는 것처럼 보이지만, 현시성을 띄는 지문이 아닌 고전이나 철학 지문의 범위에는 분명 끝이 있습니다. 이 책을 제대로 독파하며 배경지식을 쌓는다면, 이따금씩 지문을 읽어 들어가면서 앞 내용을 예측할 수 있는 내공을 쌓을 수 있게 될 것입니다.

맺으며

모국어가 아닌 언어로 대학교 수준의 텍스트를 읽고 독해해야 하는 시험은 당연히 어려울 수밖에 없습니다. 하지만 편입 수험생들은 모두가 같은 시험을 대비하느라 머리를 싸매고 어려워한다는 사실, 그리고 어려움 속에서도 고통을 참고 꾸준함을 유지하는 사람에게 좋은 결과가 찾아온다는 것은 당연하다는 점을 기억하셨으면 좋겠습니다. 저 역시 그러했습니다. 그런 과정을 거치고 합격이라는 영예를 안았습니다. 이 책을 보고 계신다면 이제 편입 준비도 후반기에 들어갔을 것이라는 생각이 듭니다. 지금껏 달려왔던 속도를 끝까지 유지할 수만 있다면, 이 책을 보는 여러분들께도 좋은 결과가 돌아올 것이라고 확신합니다. 이 책을 보는 수험생 여러분도 같은 확신을 가지고 끝까지 집중하시기 바랍니다.

차례

CONTENTS

정답 및 해설편

박문각 편입

실전 독해

PRACTICE TEST

01-20

실전 독해

01 Practice Test

Choose the one that could best complete each of the following sentences. [01~20]

(제한 시간 : 30분)

01-03

With many educators pushing for students to use resources on the Internet with class work, the federal government is now grappling with a stark disparity in access to technology, between students who have high-speed Internet at home and an estimated five million families who are without it and who are struggling to keep up.

The challenge is felt across the nation. Some students in Coachella, Calif., and Huntsville, Ala., depend on school buses that have free Wi-Fi to complete their homework. The buses are sometimes parked in residential neighborhoods overnight so that children can connect and continue studying. In cities like Detroit, Miami and New Orleans, where as many as one-third of homes do not have broadband, children crowd libraries and fast-food restaurants to use free hot spots.

The divide is driving action at the federal level. "This is what I call the homework gap, and it is the cruelest part of the digital divide," said Jessica Rosenworcel, a Democratic member of the commission who has pushed to overhaul the Lifeline program. Ms. Rosenworcel cited research showing that seven in 10 teachers now assign homework that requires web access. Yet one-third of kindergartners through 12th graders in the United States, from low-income and rural households, ______________.

01 What is the main idea of the passage?

① The educational disadvantage that some children are placed in due to lack of Wi-Fi access.

② The progressive that is being taken by some educators to bridge the technological divide.

③ The lengths children have to go to in order to get an education that adults are keeping from them.

④ The difference in life between children who have access to the Internet and those that don't.

02 Which best completes the sentence?

① don't want Wi-Fi and technology in their lives

② do not think Internet access is important

③ are unable to go online from home

④ do not even know what a computer is

03 Choose the correct statement from the following.

① Although there are places where children can go to access the Internet, they don't go to them.

② While Internet-based homework is increasing, Internet access for children doesn't match it.

③ Children can still do their homework without Wi-Fi, but it would help them.

④ This situation is only happening in a few small areas of the U.S. and not all over.

04-05

You won't be surprised to learn that you're not the only one who can't open those plastic packages that electronics, toys and so many other things seem to be encased in these days. That hard plastic packaging, also known as clamshell, oyster or blister packs, was introduced to deter shoplifting, but as a consequence of its tamper-proof features, it's also known to cause injuries when consumers try to open their purchases. In fact, according to estimates from the Consumer Product Safety Commission, every year more than 6,000 Americans are treated in emergency rooms for injuries incurred from their attempts to open plastic packaging — usually lacerations or puncture wounds (and imagine how many more of us just reached for a band-aid). The secret to blister-pack success? Put down the scissors and the knife and give your can opener a go instead. Not only is it similar to some of the special tools on the market designed to do open these packages, it actually works. And you probably have at least one in your kitchen right now.

04 **Why do people suffer injuries opening plastic packaging?**

① They use dangerous tools in order to get in that in turn hurt them.
② They don't know how to use scissors or knives correctly.
③ They hurt themselves on the hard plastic edges.
④ They do not follow the safety guidelines included.

05 **Which of the following cannot be inferred?**

① Most Americans do not report the injuries that they sustain from the packaging.
② Shoplifting decreased as a result of the introduction of hard plastic packaging.
③ People who hurt themselves on the packaging are ordered to complete a course on safety.
④ The primary reason for the packaging was not the only consequence of its creation.

01

06-07

I found that those of my friends who were admirers of Marx, Freud, and Adler, were impressed by a number of points common to these theories, and especially by their apparent explanatory power. These theories appeared to be able to explain practically everything that happened within the fields to which they referred. The study of any of them seemed to have the effect of an intellectual ________ or revelation, opening your eyes to a new truth hidden from those not yet initiated. Once your eyes were thus opened you saw confirming instances everywhere: the world was full of verifications of the theory. Whatever happened always confirmed it. Thus its truth appeared ________; and unbelievers were clearly people who did not want to see the manifest truth; who refused to see it, either because it was against their class interest, or because of their repressions which were still 'un-analysed' and crying aloud for treatment.

06 Which of the following is true, according to the passage?

① Those who did not believe these theories were admired by my friends.
② People who believed in these theories saw everything in terms of confirming them.
③ The people who refused to believe in these theories were labeled intellectuals.
④ The theories were quite limited in terms of what they could explain.

07 Which of the following fits best each blank?

① revolution − persuasive
② establishment − intuitive
③ atmosphere − doubtful
④ conversion − manifest

08-10

The polygraph, the most common lie-detection instrument, works on the assumption that the body reacts involuntarily to the stress of lying. It measures reactions such as changes in skin conductance, pulse rate, blood pressure, and breathing while the subject is asked a series of questions. [A] The questioning process can take several forms. One early version was the "relevant-irrelevant" technique, which mixed queries like "Did you murder [name of victim]?" in with stuff like "Is today Tuesday?" Lies in response to the relevant questions would supposedly make the needles jump. [B] The "comparison question" technique tries to get around this problem by making all the queries accusatory. In a sex-crime investigation, for instance, a suspect might be asked embarrassing control questions such as "Have you ever committed a sexual act you were ashamed of?" along with questions pertaining more directly to the case. [C] The idea, which has a certain devious ingenuity, is that the innocent will show a greater response to the control questions (either because they're lying or simply flustered), whereas the guilty will show a greater response to the pertinent questions (which for them are more consequential). [D]

08 Which is the best place for the following passage?

> The problem with this approach was that in such a context even an unfounded accusatory question could be stressful, producing a false positive.

① [A]
② [B]
③ [C]
④ [D]

09 What's the incorrect one from the following?

① The "relevant－irrelevant" technique had problems.
② People show stress signs even when they are innocent.
③ Guilty people respond to important questions because they know something.
④ The original version of the polygraph was not changed.

10 What is the "comparison question" technique?

① Every question is designed to make the person feel uncomfortable.
② Every question involves information about sex.
③ The questions that involve a crime are asked first.
④ The important questions are asked in groups.

11-13

Your healthcare providers will want to get an accurate picture of your blood pressure and chart what happens over time. Starting at age 20, the American Heart Association recommends a blood pressure screening at your regular healthcare visit or once every 2 years, if your blood pressure is less than 120/80 mm Hg. Your blood pressure rises with each heartbeat and falls when your heart relaxes between beats. While BP can change from minute to minute with changes in posture, exercise, stress or sleep, it should normally be less than 120/80 mm Hg (less than 120 systolic AND less than 80 diastolic) for an adult age 20 or over. About one in three (33.5%) U.S. adults has high blood pressure. If your blood pressure reading is higher than normal, your doctor may take several readings over time and/or have you monitor your blood pressure at home before diagnosing you with high blood pressure. <u>A single high reading does not necessarily mean that you have high blood pressure.</u> However, if readings stay at 140/90 mm Hg or above (systolic 140 or above OR diastolic 90 or above) over time, your doctor will likely want you to begin a treatment program. Such a program almost always includes lifestyle changes and often prescription medication for those with readings of 140/90 or higher. If, while monitoring your blood pressure, you get a systolic reading of 180 mm Hg or higher OR a diastolic reading of 110 mm HG or higher, wait a couple of minutes and take it again. If the reading is still at or above that level, you should seek immediate emergency medical treatment for a hypertensive crisis.

11 Which of the following best paraphrases the underlined sentence?

① A high reading every now and again is a warning sign that you may develop high blood pressure.

② It is necessary to seek medical attention for high blood pressure if you have a single high reading.

③ It does not go without saying that a single high reading means you have high blood pressure.

④ High blood pressure patients always show up on a single reading.

12 What's the passage mainly about?

① Preventing high blood pressure

② Developing high blood pressure

③ Treating high blood pressure

④ Diagnosing high blood pressure

13 What can be inferred about from the passage?

① High blood pressure is a serious problem for U.S. adults.

② Untreated high blood pressure will result in death.

③ If you follow a healthy lifestyle, you will not get high blood pressure.

④ Children are not susceptible to high blood pressure.

14–15

Americans spend an average of 24 minutes shopping at the supermarket, and 7 minutes more at the checkout counter. During that time the supermarket tries to achieve a balancing act — exposing the consumer to as many products as possible without ticking her off. The supermarket would like to increase the "dwell time" and have people stay even longer at the store. They employ good lighting, tempting aromas, promotions, calming music, and anything else they can think of to keep you lazily pushing your cart along all the aisles. Any technology that ultimately gets a consumer to spend more money at a supermarket or on a specific brand, will be quickly embraced by vendors and manufacturers.

14 **Which of the following is not a tactic by supermarkets to keep consumers there for longer, according to the passage?**

① Having employees engage shoppers in conversation.
② Playing music that relaxes shoppers and slows them down.
③ Pumping delicious smells through the store.
④ Advertising discounts and special deals.

15 **Which of the following means the same as the underlined?**

① while not making her angry
② when she is checking her list
③ during the moments she is not concentrating
④ as she is browsing the shelves

16-17

"It is scarcely an exaggeration to say that at present mankind as a species is demented and that nothing is so urgent upon us as the recovery of mental self-control. We call an individual insane if his ruling ideas are so much out of adjustment to his circumstances that he is a danger to himself and others. This definition of insanity seems to cover the entire human species at the present time, and it is no figure of speech but a plain statement of fact, that man has to 'pull his mind together' or perish. To perish or enter upon a phase of mature power and effort. No middle way seems open to him. He has to go up or down. He cannot stay at what he is."

— H. G. Wells.

16 What can be inferred about H. G. Wells?

① Wells was not satisfied with the state of mankind around him.
② Wells was considered insane by society.
③ Wells did not understand the human species well at all.
④ Wells was a teacher of the skill of mental self-control.

17 What is Wells urging mankind to do?

① To recover control of its senses and appreciate the world
② To accept those who are labeled insane
③ To try harder to be better humans to themselves and to others
④ To change its way of thinking so that it is more suitable to its situation

18-20

Social policy can help but is not a complete answer, said Francesco Billari, a professor of sociology and demography at Oxford. "A basic element of fertility rebound is a society with increasing gender equality," he said. "When women are in the labor market and social policy helps them and men do more child care in the household, fertility bounces up. But social policy has to be pushed by a society that ____________________."

Mr. Billari cited Italy, where the population has continued growing modestly despite traditional worries about abortion, divorce and decline. But while historically richer northern Italy once had fewer children and poorer southern Italy had large families, "now that has completely reversed," he said. Women in the richer north, he said, with more gender equality and job opportunities, are having more children than before. At the same time, women in the poorer south are having fewer children in a society with high unemployment and where there remains a "more traditional gender division of labor and lack of female participation in the work force — it's more like China," he said.

The lack of gender equality, small numbers of working women and few social policies to support them help explain why Russia, Central Europe and East Asia have generally not been able to bounce back from low fertility levels, Mr. Billari said. In general, "natalist policies" — government diktats to have more children, or appeals to patriotism, or even cash subsidies for having larger families — tend not to increase fertility very much, he said.

18 What is the best topic for the next paragraph?

① The rising status of women.

② Moving away from traditional roles.

③ Other things that can help besides social policy.

④ Persuading women to want to have families.

19 Why are women in the poorer south having fewer children?

① They want to help out the men in the labor force and having children would limit what they can do.

② The women do not want to enter the labor market, so they have no say over what happens to them.

③ The role of women is still unequal to that of men and they cannot participate in the labor force.

④ They see no opportunities for their children to grow up and attain a better standard of living.

20 Which best completes the sentence?

① is in dire straits

② that wants to increase its own fertility

③ is ready for it or demands it from politicians

④ knows what it wants and what it can get

02 Practice Test

Read the following passages and answer the questions. [01~20] (제한 시간: 30분)

01–03

Attention is not some monolithic brain process. There are different types of attention, and they use different parts of the brain. The sudden loud noise that makes you jump activates the simplest type: the startle. A chain of five neurons from your ears to your spine takes that noise and converts it into a defensive response in a mere tenth of a second — elevating your heart rate, hunching your shoulders and making you cast around to see if whatever you heard is going to pounce and eat you. This simplest form of attention requires almost no brains at all and has been observed in every studied vertebrate.

More complex attention kicks in when you hear your name called from across a room or hear an unexpected birdcall from inside a subway station. This stimulus-directed attention is controlled by pathways through the temporoparietal and inferior frontal cortex regions, mostly in the right hemisphere — areas that process the raw, sensory input, but don't concern themselves with what you should make of that sound. (Neuroscientists call this a "bottom-up" response.)

But when you actually pay attention to something you're listening to, whether it is your favorite song or the cat meowing at dinnertime, a separate "top-down" pathway comes into play. Here, the signals are conveyed through a dorsal pathway in your cortex, part of the brain that does more computation, which lets you actively focus on what you're hearing and tune out sights and sounds that aren't as immediately important. In this case, your brain works like a set of noise-suppressing headphones, with the bottom-up pathways acting as a switch to interrupt if something more urgent — say, an airplane engine dropping through your bathroom ceiling — grabs your attention.

01 **What can be inferred from the passage?**

① We have the ability to focus on what we choose to.
② There is a preprogrammed response to all stimuli we encounter.
③ The brain processes stimuli faster than we can think about it.
④ There are few animals that can think about attention from stimuli the way we do.

02 **Which of the following is incorrect according to the passage?**

① There are different levels/types of stimuli that we react to in different ways.
② The only way we pay attention to something is if it is an immediate threat to our survival.
③ The brain responds differently to stimuli from different sources, and different situations.
④ The reaction to stimuli is both a mental and physical manifestation.

03 **Why would scientists call stimulus-directed attention a 'bottom up' response?**

① It is how our brain processes all information.
② They are the type of stimuli that trigger an automated kind of recognition response, but not an interpretation of it.
③ They feel that the only way we can decide what is a valid stimuli is if it provokes a response.
④ They are the situations where there is little other information delivered to the brain, so they are not considered important by the brain.

04-07

I can only speak for what's happening in the U.K., but it seems to me that attitudes to grammar teaching here are profoundly socially divisive. Kids at fee-paying schools are likely to be given a pretty good grounding in the mechanics of language, while the others are largely taught that grammar is unimportant compared with "expressing yourself." This makes me crazy. Imagine it's the piano we are talking about. Which would be better : a) to express yourself freely on it; or b) first learn to play the thing? Of course, the difference is that people are not judged every day on their ability to play the piano. Kyle Wiens is right to point out that when young people are taught to undervalue literacy as a life skill, they are being cruelly misled. The interesting thing to me about this hoo-ha is that a company C.E.O. can still put his foot down — that it hasn't (yet) become illegal to discriminate against job applicants with poor grammar. In schools in the U.K., I imagine, such judgmentalism would not be tolerated. I recently heard an alarmist report that the British education authorities are proposing to introduce an oral version of the standard school exams (at age 16), because the traditional written method unfairly favors candidates who can read and write.

I'm sure Wiens is right that being trained to look at words on a page makes you generally more attentive to detail. The difficult thing is breaking the news to people that sometimes they are wrong, when "wrong" is a concept they have never encountered. The other day a young airline employee offered to send me "the irrelevant form." I said, "Do you mean the relevant form?" And she said, "Yes, the irrelevant form." Well, beware. There will come a day when Wiens will have no choice but to offer that girl a job.

04 **What is the opinion of the writer?**

① Knowing the rules of a language should come before trying to bend them.
② It does not matter which school you go to, you will receive the same quality of education.
③ As literacy decreases so does the quality of education.
④ The new plans for the standard school exams may be the answer to the problems.

05 **What is the meaning of the underlined final sentence?**

① Some day in the future employers will not be able to reject job candidates based on their literacy level.
② Offering both genders the same kind of job will be a thing of the past very soon.
③ It is unfortunate that intelligence levels are not taken into account in recruitment decisions.
④ We look forward to a time when a person's job status is irrelevant.

06 **Which of the following is correct, according to the passage?**

① Those people who tell youngsters that literacy is not essential are saving them a lot of time and trouble.
② The difference between fee-paying schools and other schools is that fee-paying schools do not push grammatical ability.
③ Some people have grown up being constantly told they are wrong about things.
④ Negatively judging job applicants whose grammar knowledge is lacking is thus far not punishable by law.

07 **Which is one idea for the future of British education?**

① Young people should attend classes that prepare them for both successes and failures.
② Those subjects which are better explained orally will bring in appropriate exams.
③ Students will no longer be required to write full sentences, but they can write in note form.
④ Students can give their answers in spoken form rather than the traditional written form.

08-10

Japan followed a substantially rejectionist course from its first contacts with the West in 1542 until the mid-nineteenth century. Only limited forms of modernization were permitted, such as the acquisition of firearms, and the import of Western culture, including most notably Christianity, was highly restricted. Westerners were totally expelled in the mid-seventeenth century. This rejectionist stance came to an end with the forcible opening of Japan by Commodore Perry in 1854 and the dramatic efforts to learn from the West following the Meiji Restoration in 1868. For several centuries China also attempted to bar any significant modernization or Westernization. Although Christian emissaries were allowed into China in 1601 they were then effectively excluded in 1722. Unlike Japan, China's rejectionist policy was in large part rooted in the Chinese image of itself as the Middle Kingdom and the firm belief in the superiority of Chinese culture to those of all other peoples. Chinese isolation, like Japanese isolation, was brought to an end by Western arms, applied to China by the British in the Opium War of 1839-1842. As these cases suggest, during the nineteenth century Western power made it increasingly difficult and eventually impossible for non-Western societies to adhere to purely exclusionist strategies.

08 **Which of the following is true, according to the passage?**

① China wanted nothing to do with the West because it considered itself better.

② China rejected even more strongly when Britain attempted to send firearms in.

③ Japan actively welcomed Commodore Perry into the country.

④ Non-Western societies were encouraged to be more exclusionist in their international relations.

09 **What's the main idea of the passage?**

① China and Japan collaborated to hinder the spread of Western culture at a time when the West was seeking to expand into Asia.

② China and Japan tried as hard as they could to stop the spread of Western culture, but they could not resist.

③ As much as Japan and China tried to shut out Western culture, there came a time when they could not do so for any longer.

④ Western power has never been able to fully penetrate the cultures of Japan and China.

10 **Which of the following statements about the passage does not mean the same as the others?**

① Christians were formerly prohibited from residing in China and Japan.

② The presence of Christians in China and Japan used to be highly undesirable.

③ China and Japan saw the arrival of the Christians as a sign of the downfall of their societies.

④ China and Japan did not want Christians to come into their countries in the past.

11-12

The relationship between Ricardo and Malthus began in the press, when each published essays on currency and trade issues criticizing the other. Malthus finally sent a letter to Ricardo in 1811, suggesting that since "we are mainly on the same side of the question, we might <u>supersede the necessity</u> of a long controversy in print by an amicable discussion in private." At almost the same time Ricardo was composing nearly the same note. They met a few days later and it was the beginning of a lifelong friendship. Before Ricardo's death in 1823, he wrote to Malthus, stating that despite numerous disputes, "I should not like you more than I do if you agreed in opinion with me." Only three people shared in Ricardo's will, and Malthus was one. Later Malthus announced, "I never loved anybody out of my own family so much."

11 What can be inferred from their relationship?

① Friendships are not always formed between those you see eye to eye with.
② There are not many kinds of people in the world, so we must follow the suit.
③ The best friends are always those who disagree and challenge you the most in life.
④ If you want to be friends with someone you must criticize them whenever possible.

12 Which of the following is the same as the underlined phrase in the passage?

① To give something a different purpose.
② To change the meaning of something.
③ To replace something's purpose.
④ To alter your opinion of something.

13-14

When Mozart was composing symphonies in the 18th century, little did he know he would help doctors better detect colon cancer during screenings centuries later. A small study has shown that doctors who listen to Mozart during colon colonoscopies were able to better detect pre-cancerous polyps in the colon than doctors who didn't play Mozart during the screenings. Again the study was small — only two doctors participated in the study, but the results are certainly interesting. The idea of listening to music during procedures certainly isn't new. Many doctors rock out to their favorite tunes during surgery, playing everything from The Beatles to Kenny Rogers to Kanye West while they perform procedures. I do believe that music does have a neurobiological effect on the body and if it helps surgeons to increase focus, then I am all for it. Let's just hope the rest of the OR staff shares the same taste in music as the surgeon!

13 **What's the passage mainly about?**

① The competition between doctors
② The effect of music on doctors
③ The rate of colon cancer detection
④ The outcome of using different genres

14 **What could be the problem with doctors using music, according to the passage?**

① It could bring lawsuits if something goes wrong during a procedure.
② Music could reduce the concentration of doctors and nurses.
③ Other medical staff working with the doctor may not like to work to their taste in music.
④ It is unknown whether music has any other effects on the body during surgery.

15–18

The term scientists use to describe the way the climate reacts to changes in carbon-dioxide levels is “climate sensitivity”. This is usually defined as how much hotter the Earth will get for each doubling of CO_2 concentrations. So-called equilibrium sensitivity, the commonest measure, refers to the temperature rise after allowing all feedback mechanisms to work (but without accounting for changes in vegetation and ice sheets). Carbon dioxide itself absorbs infra-red at a consistent rate. For each doubling of CO_2 levels you get roughly 1°C of warming. A rise in concentrations from preindustrial levels of 280 parts per million (ppm) to 560ppm would thus warm the Earth by 1°C. <u>If that were all there was to worry about, there would, as it were, be nothing to worry about</u>. A 1°C rise could be shrugged off. But things are not that simple, for two reasons. One is that rising CO_2 levels directly influence phenomena such as the amount of water vapour (also a greenhouse gas) and clouds that amplify or diminish the temperature rise. This affects equilibrium sensitivity directly, meaning doubling carbon concentrations would produce more than a 1°C rise in temperature. The second is that other things, such as adding soot and other aerosols to the atmosphere, add to or subtract from the effect of CO_2. All serious climate scientists agree on these two lines of reasoning. But they disagree on the size of the change that is predicted.

15 What is climate sensitivity?

① The way that the Earth is rising in temperature as CO_2 levels are being carefully reduced.

② The reaction of the Earth to attempts by climate scientists to reduce its temperature.

③ The feedback that climate scientists have given us about how to change our lifestyle to help the Earth.

④ The increase in Earth’s temperature in accordance with the rise of CO_2 levels.

16 Which of the following paraphrases the underlined sentence?

① Worrying about this will not help the problem at all.
② If only this happened, we would have no worries.
③ As this is the only worry, there are no other worries.
④ The problem is small, so this is the only worry.

17 Which of the following is true, according to the passage?

① CO_2 levels affect the temperature of the Earth through controlling water vapour and clouds.
② The Earth's temperature will continue to rise by only 1°C despite CO_2 levels.
③ CO_2 is eliminated from the atmosphere by the additional use of things in aerosol cans.
④ The reason that CO_2 levels are rising is for the reason that it cannot attract infra-red competently.

18 What is the most likely topic for the following paragraph?

① The other things that can have even bigger effects on climate change.
② The reasons why disagreements have caused climate scientists to fracture into groups.
③ Conflicting opinions on how big (or small) climate change will be.
④ The predictions that have so far been made about the necessity of climate change.

19-20

In the view of many social scientists, the more probable a theory is, the better it is, and if we have to choose between two theories which are equally strong in terms of their explanatory power, and differ only in that one is probable and the other is improbable, then we should choose the former. Popper rejects this. Science, or to be precise, the working scientist, is interested, in Popper's view, in theories with a high informative content, because such theories possess a high predictive power and are consequently highly testable. But if this is true, Popper argues, then, paradoxical as it may sound, the more improbable a theory is the better it is scientifically, because the probability and informative content of a theory vary inversely—the higher the informative content of a theory the lower will be its probability, for the more information a statement contains, the greater will be the number of ways in which it may turn out to be false. Thus the statements which are of special interest to the scientist are those with a high informative content and (consequentially) a low probability, which nevertheless come close to the truth. Informative content, which is in inverse proportion to probability, is in direct proportion to testability. Consequently the severity of the test to which a theory can be subjected, and ____________________, is all-important.

19 **What is Popper's argument, according to the passage?**

① The best theory is that which is the most informative and has the lowest probability.
② A theory is more scientific if it is informative and probable.
③ The more informative content a theory contains, the more probably it is.
④ If a theory contains the greatest amount of content, it is unlikely to be proven false.

20 **Which best completes the sentence?**

① how informative or not it is shown to be
② depending on the kinds of content it contains therein
③ as long as it can be proven to be true
④ by means of which it is falsified or corroborated

03 Practice Test

Read the following passages and answer the questions. [01~20] (제한 시간 : 30분)

01-02

With unemployment near 8 percent, many would be surprised that America runs labor shortages in several critical areas including in science, technology, engineering and math, or STEM. We haven't expanded our immigration system in more than a decade while the world has changed dramatically. ______________________: they represent 24 percent of all U.S. scientists and a remarkable 47 percent of U.S. engineers with advanced degrees. Between 1998 and 2006, U.S. patent applications from foreign-born nationals grew from 7.3 percent to 24.2 percent. With some 700,000 foreign students currently earning degrees at U.S. universities, why not offer green cards to an extra 50,000 graduates in STEM sectors? Exporting this kind of talent after graduation only hurts our global competitiveness.

01 What's the main idea of the passage?

① As foreign students continue to pour into American universities, negative attitudes to immigration increase.
② American graduates are being outdone in almost every area of expertise.
③ America needs to start exporting some of its highly-skilled graduates to increase its influence.
④ America's outdated immigration policies will hurt the country in the long run.

02 Which of the following fits the blank best?

① In order to live their American Dream, they vainly tried to settle down
② America will soon become a country that is populated by scientists
③ This matters because highly educated immigrants boost American innovation
④ The world keeps on changing, and leaving America behind in the gutter

03-05

Countries generally try to create trade policies that encourage a trade surplus. They consider this to be a favorable trade balance because it's like making a profit as a country. You'd prefer to sell more, so you can get a higher income, and have more capital for your residents. This will translate into a higher standard of living. That's because your businesses will sustain a competitive advantage by gaining the expertise in producing everything they export. They will hire more workers, reducing unemployment and generating more income for your residents.

To maintain this favorable trade balance, leaders often resort to trade protectionism. They protect domestic industries, by levying tariffs, quotas or subsidies on imports. This usually works great until other countries retaliate, and slap on their own tariffs.

In special circumstances, a trade deficit can actually be a more favorable balance of trade. It all depends on where the country is in its business cycle. For example, Hong Kong has a trade deficit, but most of its imports are raw materials which it converts to finished goods and re-exports out. Canada's slight trade deficit is a result of its strong economic growth, which allows its residents to enjoy the higher standard of living afforded by diverse imports.

On a darker side, Romania's former dictator, Nicolae Ceausescu, created a trade surplus through protectionism and forcing Romanians to save, not spend, on imports. This resulted in such a low standard of living that he was eventually forced out.

03 **According to the passage, how does trade protectionism help some nations?**

① It raises prices on premium products, bringing more income into the country.
② It gains the support of big industry for the politician who endorses it.
③ It guards domestic industries from the competition of foreign companies.
④ It keeps the jobs of the CEOs safe from more capable foreign businesspeople.

04 **Which of the following is not true?**

① Hong Kong produces things from imported raw materials and sells them out of the country again.
② Trade protectionism is used by nation leaders to improve or keep their trade surplus.
③ Canada has enjoyed a healthy economic growth which in turn has had a positive effect on its people.
④ Nicolae Ceausescu had to leave office to protect the trade of his country, Romania.

05 **What can be inferred from the passage?**

① The trade deficit in Hong Kong and Canada is the ideal situation for a country.
② If every country follows trade protectionism, the standard of living of all will increase.
③ A favorable trade balance for one country suits all parties concerned.
④ Hong Kong has not tried to reverse its trade deficit.

06-08

In resenting progress and change, a man lays himself open to censure. I suppose the explanation of anyone's defending anything as rudimentary and cramped as a Pullman berth is that things are associated with an earlier period in one's life and that this period in retrospect seems a happy one. People who favor progress and improvements are apt to be people who have had a tough enough time without any extra inconveniences. Reactionaries who pout at innovations are apt to be well-heeled sentimentalists who had the breaks. Yet for all that, there is always a subtle danger in life's refinements, a dim degeneracy in progress. I have just been refining the room in which I sit, yet I sometimes doubt that a writer should refine or improve his workroom by so much as a dictionary: one thing leads to another and the first thing you know he has a stuffed chair and is fast asleep in it. Half a man's life is devoted to what he calls improvements, yet the original had some quality which is lost in the process. There was a fine natural spring of water on this place when I bought it. Our drinking water had to be lugged in a pail, from a wet glade of alder and tamarack. I visited the spring often in those first years, and had friends there — a frog, a woodcock, and an eel which had churned its way all the way up through the pasture creek to enjoy the luxury of pure water. In the normal course of development, the spring was rocked up, fitted with a concrete curb, a copper pipe, and an electric pump. I have visited it only once or twice since. This year my only gesture was the purely perfunctory one of sending a sample to the state bureau of health for analysis.

06 **How does the author feel about the idea of progress and change according to the passage?**

① The author is in favor of progress and change.
② The author likes the idea of progress but dislikes change.
③ The author is open to both progress and change.
④ The author accepts their happening but does not fully agree with them.

07 **Which of the following is true according to the passage?**

① The author is a very wealthy person.
② There are few things in the world that remain unchanged.
③ The unique value that made us like something gets lost in the change of progress.
④ The cost of progress and change is higher than most of us believe it to be.

08 **What is the meaning of the underlined phrase?**

① The majority of people like change and progress, so those opposed to it are shunned.
② Those who dislike change and progress are kept from expressing their opinions.
③ When people speak out against new ideas they are often silenced.
④ There are many more people who like the idea of change than those who oppose its progress.

09-11

Ethnic minorities will soon account for 30 percent of all consumer purchases. No wonder they are increasingly important to advertisers. Nearly half of all Fortune 1000 companies have some kind of ethnic marketing campaign. Nonetheless, minorities are still underrepresented in advertising agencies. African Americans, who are over 10 percent of the total workforce, are only 5 percent of the advertising industry. Minorities are underrepresented in ads as well, about 87 percent of people in mainstream magazine ads are white, about 3 percent are African American, most likely appearing as athletes or musicians, and less than 1 percent are Hispanic or Asian. As the spending power of minorities increases, so does marketing segmentation. Mass marketing aimed at a universal audience doesn't work so well in a multicultural society, but cable television, the Internet, custom publishing, and direct marketing lend themselves very well to this segmentation. The multiculturalism that we see in advertising is about money, of course, not about social justice.

09 **What is the main idea of the paragraph?**

① Ethnic minorities should be represented more in advertising.

② African Americans do not need to be considered when inventing an advertising campaign.

③ Ethnic minorities are outraged that they are ignored.

④ The Internet is leading the way in multicultural advertising.

10 **What can be inferred about mass marketing?**

① It will become much easier to target consumers across cultures.

② Multicultural societies are forcing its collapse.

③ It will become more polarized as minorities gain wealth.

④ It does not have any effect on minorities.

11 **Choose the true statement from the following.**

① Ethnic minorities already account for nearly half of consumer purchases.

② Three quarters of the Fortune 1000 companies have an ethnic marketing campaign.

③ African Americans are only just short of the same representation as white people in mainstream magazine ads.

④ Hispanics are represented less than African Americans in mainstream magazine ads.

12-14

McSorley's bar is short, accommodating approximately ten elbows, and is shored up with iron pipes. It is to the right as you enter. To the left is a row of armchairs with their stiff backs against the wainscoting. The chairs are rickety; when a fat man is sitting in one, it squeaks like new shoes every time he takes a breath. The customers believe in sitting down; if there are vacant chairs, no one ever stands at the bar. Down the middle of the room is a row of battered tables. Their tops are always sticky with spilled ale. In the centre of the room stands the belly stove, which has an isinglass door and is exactly like the stoves in Elevated stations. All winter Kelly keeps it red hot. 'Warmer you get, drunker you get," he says. Some customers prefer mulled ale. They keep their mugs on the hob until the ale gets as hot as coffee. A sluggish cat named Minnie sleeps in a scuttle beside the stove. The floor boards are warped, and here and there a hole has been patched with a flattened-out soup can. The back room looks out on a blind tenement court. In this room are three big, round dining room tables. The kitchen is in one corner of the room; Mike keeps a folding boudoir screen around the gas range, and pots, pans, and paper bags of groceries are stored on the mantelpiece. While he peels potatoes, he sits with early customers at a table out front, holding a dishpan in his lap and talking as he peels. The fare in McSorley's is plain, cheap, and well cooked. Mike's specialties are goulash, frankfurters, and sauerkraut, and hamburgers <u>blanketed with fried onions</u>. He scribbles his menus in chalk on a slate which hangs in the bar-room and constantly misspells four dishes out of five. There is no waiter. During the lunch hour, if Mike is too busy to wait on the customers, they grab plates and help themselves out of the pots on the range.

12 Which of the following statements is incorrect, according to the passage?

① Mike likes to get friendly with his customers.
② The food on the menu at McSorley's is fancy.
③ Mike trusts his customers to help themselves.
④ The place is not the cleanest and tidiest of bars.

13 Which of the following means the same as the underlined phrase?

① warmed by fried onions
② covered completely with fried onions
③ cooked with fried onions
④ sautéed with fried onions

14 What can you infer from the passage?

① Mike hates working at McSorley's and is looking for an appropriate time to leave.
② The customers at McSorley's are always changing; nobody comes back.
③ McSorley's is a homely and comfortable place to go.
④ Mike is hoping to expand McSorley's into a bigger space.

15-17

The Veblen effect, which is named after the scholar who came up with the theory, is a form of irrational consumption. The Veblen effect is the most complex of the three "nonfunctional" external effects on demand. It affects the sociological or psychological behavior of the consumer. A basic summary of the Veblen effect might be when a consumer's demand (or consumption) of a certain good is increased when the price also is increased. This is against traditional theory of rationality. However, the consumer perceives that the good brings a higher utility at a higher price. For instance, say there are two pairs of very similar shoes in a store; everything is the same about the shoes except one pair has a small "Jordan" symbol on it. Also, the pair of shoes with the "Jordan" symbol has a price that is significantly higher than the other pair of similar shoes. A consumer who buys the shoes with the "Jordan" symbol is displaying the Veblen effect. They are willing to pay a much higher price for essentially the same product, because they think they will get a higher utility. This is just one example; there could be many more examples where consumers are overspending on products because they hope to get a higher utility from having the "cool" thing. This is irrational consumption and spurs from the individual hoping to "show off" that they have a more expensive product, even though the product may serve the same function of a much cheaper product.

15 What is the purpose of this passage?

① To explain why you should buy the cheaper product.

② To inform the readers of their irrational consumption.

③ To show that there is logic in everything, even those things that seem random.

④ To explain how irrational consumption has a rational explanation.

16 Which of the following is correct according to the passage?

① People will always do the irrational thing with consumption practices.

② People will buy things if they feel they have an intrinsic value of some sort.

③ Once aware of the Veblen effect, people will not make irrational purchases.

④ There is little support for the hypothesis proposed by Veblen.

17 Why do people buy irrationally according to the passage?

① They want to have the best.

② They do not think that the two products are of equal quality.

③ They want to spend more money whenever possible.

④ They believe that the product they are buying has some intangible value the other lacks.

18-20

Apart from cases of miraculous conception, whether fertilised in utero or in vitro, the trigger for human life has been, until recently, the introduction of a male's sperm into a female's egg. The introduction of the sperm initiates a process by which the egg then begins the process of division — syngamy — normally incorporating and combining genetic material from both the egg and sperm. For the majority of human history fertilisation of an egg has occurred through the mechanism of sexual intercourse. More recently, advances in reproductive technology have allowed us to initiate human life by inserting sperm directly into an egg in vitro — that is, outside the human body. The fertilised egg is then allowed to develop for a period of time before being implanted in a womb — after which the normal process of growth and development continues in utero. It has also become possible to cause the egg cells of human beings to begin dividing without first being fertilised by a sperm cell. The process, partheno- genesis, occurs naturally in many plant and insect species. It can be induced in mammalian egg cells using either an electrical or chemical stimulus. Where parthenogenesis is employed and human life begins, the subsequent embryo possesses only the genetic material contained in the nucleus of the egg prior to stimulation.

18 **What is the best title for the passage?**

① Reproduction, now and then
② The way to have a baby
③ How we make offspring
④ Reproductive methods today

19 **What can be inferred from the passage?**

① There has been a large amount of work and research in reproduction.
② Many people choose to have in vitro babies now.
③ There is no reason to use in vitro fertilization except when you are single.
④ Many different methods of parthenogenesis can be used by all species when needed.

20 **Which of the following is incorrect according to the passage?**

① In vitro fertilization is an alternative method of fertilization.
② Parthenogenesis is a normal method of reproduction for humans.
③ In utero is the natural method of reproduction for humans.
④ There are several methods available to humans to reproduce, even without a partner.

04 Practice Test

Read the following passages and answer the questions. [01~20] (제한 시간 : 30분)

01-03

What is special relativity? The theory is based on two key concepts. First, the natural world allows no "privileged" frames of reference. As long as an object is moving in a straight line at a constant speed (that is, with no acceleration), the laws of physics are the same for everyone. It's a bit like when you look out a train window and see an adjacent train appear to move—but is it moving, or are you? It can be hard to tell. Einstein recognized that if the motion is perfectly uniform, it's literally impossible to tell—and identified this as a central principle of physics. Second, light travels at an unvarying speed of 186,000 miles a second. No matter how fast an observer is moving or how fast a light-emitting object is moving, a measurement of the speed of light always yields the same result. Starting from these two postulates, Einstein showed that space and time are intertwined in ways that scientists had never previously realized.

[A] What's more, your friend's rocket will appear shorter than your own. If your rocket speeds up, your mass and that of the rocket will increase.

[B] Through a series of thought experiments, Einstein demonstrated that the consequences of special relativity are often counterintuitive—even startling.

[C] If you're zooming along in a rocket and pass a friend in an identical but slower-moving rocket, for example, you'll see that your friend's watch is ticking along more slowly than yours (physicists call this "time dilation").

[D] The faster you go, the heavier things become and the more your rocket will resist your efforts to make it go faster. Einstein showed that ______________.

01 What is the passage mainly about?

① Einstein's discovery of the speed of light
② The laws of physics when it comes to speed
③ The central concepts of special relativity
④ The lack of influence of humans on science

02 Choose the most logical order of the following sentences.

① [B] – [C] – [A] – [D]
② [C] – [B] – [A] – [D]
③ [C] – [A] – [D] – [B]
④ [B] – [D] – [A] – [C]

03 Which best completes the sentence?

① space and time are not as closely related as previously thought
② nothing that has a mass can ever reach the speed of light
③ all other theories that came before his were wrong
④ the speed of light cannot change unless one starts to move faster

04-05

Money isn't everything. That's the idea behind the United Nations' Human Development Index. It incorporates measures for income, life expectancy and education into a single development score, which is designed to give a holistic sense of how a country is doing. The latest report is published today, providing a good opportunity to chart progress over the past 25 years. Rwanda has made the most progress, which is all the more impressive given that its level of development fell during the genocide of 1994. Rwandans can now expect to live almost 32 years longer than in 1990, and spend twice as long at school. China comes in at number two. Its score today is roughly what South Korea's was in 1990. Happily, all 142 countries with complete data (for a few places, such as Ethiopia and Somalia, some data are missing) are more developed than they were a quarter of a century ago, except unlucky Swaziland, which has been devastated by AIDS.

04 **How is the United Nations' Human Development Index different?**

① Its purpose is to encourage those nations that traditionally land at the bottom.
② It is designed to determine the happiness level of a country regardless of money.
③ It measures the progress a country has made in ways other than just getting rich.
④ It removes economic prosperity from the equation entirely to measure development.

05 **Why is Rwanda impressive?**

① There are still factions in the country that hark back to the civil war of 1994 and fondly remember a time when progress was curtailed.
② Just before the civil war, Rwanda was at the forefront of development while after 1994 it had dropped to the bottom.
③ The 1994 civil war was an attempt to prevent any progress in this staunchly conservative and religious country.
④ During its civil war in 1994, its development dropped drastically, but it has managed to turn things around again.

06-07

When linguists claim to find the same kinds of linguistic gadgets in language after language, it is not just because they expect languages to have subjects and so they label as a 'subject' the first kind of phrase they see that resembles an English subject. ___________, if a linguist examining a language for the first time calls a phrase a 'subject' using one criterion based on English subjects — say, denoting the agent role of action verbs — the linguist soon discovers that other criteria, like agreeing with the verb in person and number and occurring before the object, will be true of that phrase as well. It is these correlations among the properties of a linguistic thing across languages that make it scientifically meaningful to talk about subjects and objects and nouns and verbs and auxiliaries and inflections in languages from Abaza to Zyrian.

06 What is the main idea of the passage?

① Language is a complex structured system of words.
② It is meaningful to explore the correlation among linguistic traits through language.
③ Human language is unique in comparison to other forms of communication.
④ The study of language structure is a difficult and scientific pursuit.

07 Which word fits the blank?

① Nevertheless
② Therefore
③ Rather
④ However

08-10

Son preference, missing girls, sex selection: We may seek to label these Chinese or Indian issues, but they exist here in America. The extent of sex-selective practices in the U.S. is hard to assess, since it's rarely something people will admit to doing. But we can make an educated guess by observing alterations in expected sex ratios. If nature has its way, women will likely give birth to 100 girls for every 102 to 106 boys (for a ratio of 1.02 to 1.06 boys per girl). And among first-time parents in the U.S., that's exactly what we see.

However, as birth order rises, apparently so does selection — at least, in certain ethnic groups. With 2000 U.S. Census data, researchers investigating Korean, Chinese, and Indian communities found that, after having one girl, parents have as many as 1.17 boys per girl when their next child is born. With two girls at home, the ratio goes up to 1.51 boys per girl for the third child (meaning 151 boys are born for each 100 girls). These skewed ratios aren't present among other ethnic groups in America.

In practice, sex selection means more sons. In most cultures, there's a preference for male babies. Whether the motivation is economic (because sons mean higher income potential), religious (because sons perform sacred rites), social (because sons confer status), or a messy mix of the above, son preference fuels the desire to take control of formerly unalterable aspects of impending parenthood. Obviously, sex preference is a problem. It requires adherence to the fallacy that sons and daughters are biologically limited in what they can do and who they can be. <u>People lusting after a son hardly have a hairdresser in mind</u>. Likewise, the daughter dream is about playing princess, not baseball. Moreover, desperately wanting a specific sex requires us to believe in and thus perpetuate the notion of two genders.

Responses from our own surveys, individual interviews and focus groups among Asian Americans indicate sex preference is alive in America. While respondents generally didn't have first-hand experience with sex selection in the U.S., 96 percent felt that parents treat boys and girls differently, with boys getting a way better deal. Sex selection may be, to paraphrase one respondent, the operationalization of son preference, but the preference came first — and left unaddressed, isn't going anywhere.

08 **What's the main idea of the passage?**

① Sex selection is decreasing in most communities in the US.

② The current prevalence of sex selection in the U.S.

③ The different abilities of sons and daughters.

④ Sons and daughters should be brought up in different ways.

09 **What can you infer from the passage?**

① A wider spread of communities is going to be surveyed.

② Increasingly, girls are being treated more fairly than boys.

③ Sex selection does not exist in the US, only China or India.

④ Not every couple has the same reason for preferring a son.

10 **Which of the following most closely resembles the underlined sentence?**

① Sons do not want to be hairdressers whatever their parents might want.

② Those people who want a son do not envisage a hairdressing career for his future.

③ If your mind desires a hairdresser, you should raise your son accordingly.

④ People who become hairdressers do not think about their career when they are children.

11–12

The Japanese language contains many other examples of language that do not translate culturally into English. Names, for example, are often not used in Japanese if there is some way to avoid it. Relationships or occupations are frequently used to refer to people instead. A Japanese learner of English in America may experience culture shock at the idea of calling a teacher by his or her name rather than just calling that person "teacher." These can be seen as cultural manifestations of the Whorfian Hypothesis.
Culture and language are bound together so tightly that learning a new language requires learning a new culture and thus a new way of viewing the world. Interestingly, some English teachers in Japan do not use these English cultural norms in class, believing that exposing the students to a different culture will cause them culture shock. Thus, "brother" is taught as a word in combination with "elder/older" and "younger," after which "brother" by itself may be encountered less frequently than phrases that match the Japanese cultural norm (i.e. "elder brother") even though in American English "brother" by itself would be far more common.

11 **What can be inferred from the passage?**

① Learning a second language without its culture can be very challenging.
② Language learning is not possible for everyone.
③ Different languages do not have the same words for the same thing.
④ Japanese culture is very unique compared to other cultures.

12 **Why do people get culture shock from learning language?**

① Because they don't understand why certain words are used for things.
② Because they have never experienced a different culture before.
③ Because language learning tends to force its culture on the learner.
④ Because their teachers force their own cultural beliefs on them when they are learning.

13–14

I want only to mention very briefly before starting with the discussion of Luther's theology, that Luther as a person was a typical representative of the "authoritarian character". Having been brought up by an unusually severe father and having experienced little love or security as a child, his personality was torn by a constant __________ towards authority; he hated it and rebelled against it, while at the same time he admired it and tended to submit to it. During his whole life there was always one authority against which he was opposed and another which he admired — his father and his superiors in the monastery in his youth; the Pope and the princes later on. He was filled with an extreme feeling of aloneness, powerlessness, wickedness, but at the same time with a passion to dominate. He was tortured by doubts as only a compulsive character can be, and was constantly seeking for something which would give him inner ________ and relieve him from this torture of uncertainty.

13 Which of the following is the best idea for the next passage?

① The relationship between Luther and various members of his family
② The negative effects of religion on Luther
③ The controlling and dominant temperament of Luther
④ The teenage years that cemented Luther's personality

14 Which of the following fits best each blank?

① dichotomy — certainty
② confusion — composure
③ equanimity — instability
④ ambivalence — security

15-17

Perhaps the most infamous of all Internet cons is the Nigerian money transfer, or advance fee fraud. Virtually everyone with an e-mail address has received a come-on for this con at some point. Someone from Nigeria (or another African country), perhaps a relative of a recently deposed ruler, informs you that he needs your assistance in a very important matter. It seems that this deposed ruler has millions of dollars stashed away in a secure bank account. However, he can't access any of this money without paying certain fees, bribes and fines to Nigerian authorities. <u>That's where the victim comes in</u> — <u>to provide money to pay these costs</u>. The victim is assured that once the costs are paid, the government will release the money and he will receive a huge return on his investment. Often the e-mail promises a large percentage of the total sum.

Anyone who has actually sent money to these con artists will soon find that other fees crop up. The money may get held up at the border, so more money is needed to bribe the customs officials. The con artists often request personal information such as Social Security numbers and copies of passports. This goes on and on, playing on one of the most nefarious aspects of long-term cons — once the victim has spent a significant amount of money, he believes if he just spends a little more then he'll get it all back. With so much money already invested, most people find it very difficult to walk away. Some people have been lured to the country of origin, kidnapped and held for ransom. There is even a documented murder related to such a case. The country of Nigeria is notorious for a combination of poverty and lax law enforcement, especially with regards to financial scams. The section of Nigerian law relating to fraud is 419, so these scams are sometimes referred to as 419 scams. But the scams can originate from anywhere, as our example above shows.

15 What's the idea of the passage?

① Why people believe Nigerian money scams.
② Who the Nigerian money scams target.
③ How Nigerian money scams work.
④ How money scams are created.

16 Why do the victims of the scams keep sending money, according to the passage?

① They have invested too much money not to be able to walk away easily.
② They do not want to admit they have made a mistake.
③ They want to learn how to do their own scams.
④ By sending money, they will lead police to the scammers.

17 Which of the following means the same as the underlined sentence?

① It costs a lot to take part in a money scam.
② The victim is provided with money for his worries.
③ The victim comes to the country to receive money.
④ The victim's role is to pay to get the money out of the country.

18-20

Justice as fairness is not a complete contract theory. For it is clear that the contractarian idea can be extended to the choice of more or less an entire ethical system, that is, to a system including principles for all the virtues and not only for justice. Now for the most part I shall consider only principles of justice and others closely related to them; I make no attempt to discuss the virtues in a systematic way. Obviously if justice as fairness succeeds reasonably well, a next step would be to study the more general view suggested by the name "rightness as fairness." But even this wider theory fails to embrace all moral relationships, since it would seem to include only our relations with other persons and to leave out of account how we are to conduct ourselves toward animals and the rest of nature. I do not contend that the contract notion offers a way to approach these questions which are certainly of the first importance; and I shall have to put them aside. We must recognize ______________________ of justice as fairness and of the general type of view that it exemplifies. How far its conclusions must be revised once these other matters are understood cannot be decided in advance.

18 **Which word or phrase fits the blank?**

① the deep justification
② such a standard
③ the limited scope
④ the general goal

19 **Why does the wider theory the author mentions fail to include all moral relationships?**

① It presupposes only the interactions of human kind and not the extended ones that merely involve humans.

② The author feels justice cannot hope to encompass such a large volume of interactions.

③ The theory that the author speaks of can only be applied to situations both parties are moral.

④ The author feels that the rest of the world lacks the necessary morality needed to understand the complexity of justice.

20 **What can be inferred from the passage?**

① Morality and justice are two unrelated positions.

② The only true justice is that of the moral kind.

③ There are many different justice and fairness that do not always coincide.

④ Justice is not always fair to those you think it should be.

05 Practice Test

Read the following passages and answer the questions. [01~20] (제한 시간 : 30분)

01-03

Research has been performed with the intention of discovering how pigeons, after being transported, can find their way back from distant places they have never visited before. Most researchers believe that homing ability is based on a "map and compass" model, with the compass feature allowing birds to orient and the map feature allowing birds to determine their location relative to a goal site (home loft). While the compass mechanism appears to rely on the sun, the map mechanism has been highly debated. Some researchers believe that the map mechanism relies on the ability of birds to detect the Earth's magnetic field. It is true that birds can detect a magnetic field, to help them find their way home. Scientists have found that on top of a pigeon's beak a large number of particles of iron are found which remain aligned to north like a man-made compass; ______________________________.
A light-mediated mechanism that involves the eyes and is lateralized has been examined somewhat, but recent developments have implicated the trigeminal nerve in magnetoception.

01 What is the main idea of the passage?

① The way that when traveling from an unknown place to home, they know the direction.
② The difference between pigeons and other birds who cannot travel without extra help.
③ The mechanism that allows pigeons to orient themselves around their homes.
④ Differing research on what goes on inside a pigeon's head when it is lost.

02 Which of the following fits in the blank best?

① thus, it acts as a compass which helps a pigeon in determining its home
② therefore, it causes the beak to act in a different way from that for which it was intended
③ so, being aligned is the most important technique for a beak to perform this function
④ consequently, it does not have the required things in order to work correctly

03 What is the probable topic of the next part of the passage?

① The light that comes from a pigeon's eyes when it begins to fly.
② The relationship between a pigeon's eyes and where it lives.
③ Chief developments that have taken place in the travel of pigeon.
④ The latest research that has taken place concerning magnetoception.

04-06

"Great movie quotes become part of our cultural vocabulary." So said Jean Pickler Firstenberg, director and CEO of the American Film Institute, when in 2005 AFI released its list of the top 100 memorable movie lines. The jury assembled (made up of directors, actors, screenwriters, critics, historians, and others in the creative community) to select the top quotations was instructed to make their picks based on a quotation's "cultural impact" and legacy. It says something about American culture and priorities that a lot more of us can recite lines voiced in movies released fifty years ago than can tell you what our United States senator said this week, last week … ever.

When it comes to movie language, fiction is often more powerful than reality. Think about it. A lot more people know that Arnold Schwarzenegger delivered a defiant "I'll be back" (AFI rank #37) guarantee in the blockbuster film *The Terminator* than know that General Douglas MacArthur declared "I shall return" as he fled the Philippines from the advancing Japanese in that blockbuster military conflict World War II. Other than the infamous <u>"If it doesn't fit, you must acquit,"</u> no real courtroom language is more immediately recognizable than the make-believe "You can't handle the truth" (#29) outburst by Jack Nicholson in the Aaron Sorkin-penned *A Few Good Men*. How many people know that "Keep your friends close but your enemies closer" from *The Godfather* (#58) is almost identical to what philosopher John Stuart Mill wrote 150 years ago and what Machiavelli advised almost 500 years ago? Surely not many.

04 **What does the underlined phrase mean?**

① If the trial doesn't fit into your life, don't take part in it.
② If an acquittal is what you want, you will get it.
③ If something doesn't add up, seek a retrial.
④ If the facts don't make sense, the person on trial must be set free.

05 **What can be inferred about American culture?**

① Americans find it easier to remember movie stories than real stories.
② Senators have an appalling reputation in American society.
③ Movies are the sole priority in American lives.
④ The general public are more interested in movies than politics.

06 **How were the top quotes picked?**

① By choosing great films with lots of suitable quotations.
② By examining what legacy the movie the quotation had come from had left.
③ By how many people could remember he quotation when asked.
④ By how much the quotation had affected culture and how people remembered it.

07-09

People who have a fixed mindset believe that their abilities are basically static. If you are someone with a fixed mindset, you tend to avoid challenges, because if you fail, you fear that others will see your failure as an indication of your true ability and see you as a loser (just as a bad first taste of wine leads you to reject the bottle). You feel threatened by negative feedback, because it seems as if the critics are saying they're better than you, positioning themselves at a level of natural ability higher than yours. You try not to be seen exerting too much effort. (People who are really good don't need to try that hard, right?) Think about tennis player John McEnroe as a young star — he had great natural talent but was not keen on rigorous practice or self-improvement.

In contrast, people who have a growth mindset believe that abilities are like muscles — they can be built up with practice. That is, with concerted effort, you can make yourself better at writing or managing or listening to your spouse. With a growth mindset, you tend to accept more challenges despite the risk of failure. (After all, when you try and fail to lift more weight at the gym, you don't worry that everybody will mock you as a "born weakling.") You seek out "stretch" assignments at work. And you're more inclined to accept criticism, because ultimately it makes you better. You may not be as good as others right now, but you're thinking long-term, in a tortoise-versus-hare kind of way. Think Tiger Woods, who won eight major championships faster than anyone in history and then decided his swing needed an overhaul.

07 What is the passage about?

① Learning to accept that whatever your mindset, fixed or growth, you will be able to succeed in life.

② Trying to make sure that your fixed mindset is able to take in the positives of a growth mindset.

③ How changing your fixed mindset into a more relaxed growth mindset can help you to be more successful.

④ The difference in behavior between those who have a fixed mindset and those that have a growth mindset.

08 What is the characteristic of a growth mindset?

① Somebody that criticizes others for fear that they are being criticized themselves.

② Someone that does not fully comprehend quite how talented they are although others can see it clearly.

③ Someone who knows they are inferior to others but does not feel threatened when the show their superiority.

④ Somebody who makes mistakes and is willing to accept criticism in order to improve themselves.

09 Which of the following is incorrect, according to the passage?

① Regardless of their mindset, people know that their hard work will pay off down the line.

② Even after being amazingly successful, Tiger Woods did not rest on his laurels and sought to improve himself.

③ A fixed mindset person has low self-esteem and constantly feels they are being judged on their failures.

④ Avoiding doing new things is a way for those with a fixed mindset to avoid failing.

10-12

2013 was a tough year for Claudia F. as her grandma passed away, she graduated from college, and was struggling finding out who she was in the real world, so she began to shop in order to bring comfort in this new life. Now a mother of three, she says that at the time she wanted to fill a void inside of her and she didn't know what she was doing. Her weekend shopping trips soon escalated into an obsession that saw her put $30,000 on credit cards in 6 or 8 months. As she bought more and more, she would hide purchases in her husband's car or in a closet and forget they were even there as if they meant nothing to her. When the couple's home modification loan application was rejected, Claudia's marriage hit the rocks ______________________________. She realized how much potential danger she had put her family in financially. Claudia overcame her obsession by coming to the realization that who she was and what she had was enough. Now, she says she has recovered and spends frugally. Shulman remarks that shopping addiction appears due to many things. Most people have money issues but it is usually a traumatic event, such as an unhappy marriage, losing a job, or having unwanted children that triggers addiction. The shopping addiction begins because it is the only time when sufferers experience control in their lives. They can forget all their worries and focus on buying whatever they want, and on buying it, they feel like they have achieved something. In order to get to the bottom of an addiction, specialized help is needed. Any kind of addiction cannot be gotten rid of by simple abstinence, but we need to find out what is essentially causing it.

10 Which of the following best completes the sentence?

① as she was forced to face up to what she had done
② when her husband refused to stand by her
③ since she had not trusted him with her secret
④ and they lost their home in an instant

11 What can you infer about a shopping addict?

① They are very lonely people.
② They care deeply about the product before buying it but then often forget about it.
③ They don't care about their family or themselves enough to stop shopping.
④ A shopping addict can cured easily; they just need to stay away from shops or the Internet.

12 Why does Shulman think people become addicts?

① They have been severely depressed for a long time and it is the only time when they feel better.
② A traumatic event in our lives can make us feel that it is the only thing we can control.
③ They have been denying themselves something for too long.
④ They have been addicted to a number of things in their lives and this is the next stage.

13–16

The impulse of the atmosphere to seek equilibrium was first suspected by Edmond Halley and elaborated upon in the eighteenth century by his fellow Briton George Hadley, who saw that rising and falling columns of air tended to produce "cells" (known ever since as "Hadley cells"). Though a lawyer by profession, Hadley had a keen interest in the weather (he was, after all, English) and also suggested a link between his cells, the Earth's spin, and the apparent deflections of air that give us our trade winds. However, it was an engineering professor at the École Polytechnique in Paris, Gustave-Gaspard de Coriolis, who worked out the details of these interactions in 1835, and thus we call it the Coriolis effect. The Earth revolves at a brisk 1,041 miles an hour at the equator, though as you move toward the poles the rate slopes off considerably, to about 600 miles an hour in London or Paris, for instance. <u>The reason for this is self-evident when you think about it</u>. If you are on the equator the spinning Earth has to carry you quite a distance — about 40,000 kilometers — to get you back to the same spot. If you stand beside the North Pole, however, you may need travel only a few feet to complete a revolution, yet in both cases it takes twenty-four hours to get you back to where you began. Therefore, it follows that the closer you get to the equator the faster you must be spinning.

13 **What is the main idea of the passage?**

① The confusion of the Earth when it is not equal.
② The research that went into discovering the Earth's tendencies.
③ The origin and physical principle behind Coriolis effect
④ The simplicity of how the Earth has steadied itself.

14 **Which of the following means the same as the underlined?**

① Having some awareness about this is important.
② It is quite obvious if you stop and consider it.
③ The whys and wherefores of the process is no longer a mystery.
④ The clarity of the issue comes from thinking about it.

15 **What is the Coriolis effect concerned with?**

① The speed at which the Earth spins
② The distance between places on Earth
③ The wind that affects trade routes
④ The reaction of the air to the Earth

16 **What can be inferred from the passage?**

① Air tends to rotate to the left in the Northern Hemisphere.
② As a result of the Coriolis effect, the Earth revolves around the sun.
③ The Coriolis effect is caused by the Earth's rotation.
④ Earth rotates faster at the poles than it does at the equators.

17-20

Allen, professor of psychology at the University of Virginia, and his colleagues followed 184 youth from a public middle school in the Southeast, which included kids from both urban and suburban neighborhoods. They interviewed the teens' parents as well as other adolescents that the youth identified as their closest friends annually for three years, starting when the participants were around 13. The authors followed up again when they were aged 20 to 23.

"What we're finding is that the path is not straightforward, it's more <u>like a tightrope walk</u> between trying to connect well with peers on one side and avoiding getting swept up into peer influences toward deviant behavior like delinquency and drug use on the other," says Allen.

Indeed, the study showed that teens who best resisted peer pressure during junior high were less likely to engage in criminal behavior or to have alcohol or other drug problems. Unfortunately, this ability to resist peer pressure can also be isolating; this same group also had fewer and weaker friendships as adults.

Those who had the strongest interactions as adults, not surprisingly, were teens who walked a middle ground, remaining open to peer influence, but not allowing themselves to be overwhelmed by the pressure to conform. "Teens who can manage that well have strong close friendships as adults," says Allen, "They're better at negotiating disagreements with romantic partners when we observed them doing that. They are less likely to have problems with alcohol and substance use and less likely to engage in criminal behavior."

17 What was the subject of the research?

① The effect of taking drugs on the minds of teenagers and adults.
② The relationship between dealing with peer pressure as a teenager and interactions as adults.
③ The way that substance abuse of teenagers corresponds with that of their friends or parents.
④ The similarity between the friendships that one has as a teenager and then as an adult.

18 Which group of teenagers turned out to be better-adjusted adults?

① Those whom the popular kids ignored but did not seek out to negatively attack.
② The teenagers who maintained friendships amongst those that turned their backs on delinquency.
③ The ones that were able to resist peer pressure but not the bullying that would accompany it.
④ Those that neither bowed to peer pressure nor assertively rejected it.

19 What does the underlined phrase mean?

① It's like being in a circus for those that choose to participate.
② There is a very narrow path that they have to find to survive.
③ As they grow up, it becomes more difficult to find your place.
④ Walking between groups of influences is exhilarating.

20 Choose the incorrect statement from the following.

① The research took into account teenagers from different backgrounds.
② The teenagers were interviewed at different points in their lives.
③ The participants were visited and asked questions three times per year.
④ The teenagers' were taken from one large area of the country.

06 Practice Test

Read the following passages and answer the questions. [01~20] (제한 시간 : 30분)

01-03

Irony, history, and racism all painfully intertwine in our past and present, and they all come together in *Huck Finn*. Because racism is endemic to our society, a book like *Huck Finn*, which brings the problem to the surface, can explode like a hand grenade in a literature classroom accustomed to the likes of *Macbeth or Great Expectations* — works which exist at a safe remove from the lunchroom or the playground. If we lived in a world in which racism had been eliminated generations before, teaching *Huck Finn* would be a piece of cake. Unfortunately that's not the world we live in. The difficulties we have teaching this book reflect the difficulties we continue to confront in our classrooms and our nation. As educators, it is incumbent upon us to teach our students to decode irony, to understand history, and to be repulsed by racism and bigotry wherever they find it. But this is the task of a lifetime. It's unfair to force one novel to bear the burden — alone — of addressing these issues and solving these problems. But *Huck Finn* — and you — can make a difference.

01 What's the topic of the passage?

① The importance of teaching *Huck Finn*, especially considering the issues in the world today.
② The role that *Huck Finn* played in driving racism out of the classrooms.
③ The difficulties that teachers face in teaching *Huck Finn* to students who don't care.
④ The avoidable problems that *Huck Finn* raises in society today.

02 Which of the following statements cannot be inferred from the passage?

① *Huck Finn* sometimes causes great emotions in schoolchildren.
② Teaching *Huck Finn* can go a little way towards teaching children to reject racism.
③ *Huck Finn* is often considered an inferior novel to the likes of Shakespeare or Dickens.
④ Racism still exists today.

03 Which of the following is true, according to the passage?

① Teaching *Huck Finn* is difficult because the issues in the book still exist today.
② Any educator that knows the book well can teach it quite easily.
③ Teachers should not get involved in society's problems, but stick to teaching facts.
④ The stories of Shakespeare reflect the real life of children.

04–05

What are the things that historians can learn from journalists? Storytelling : How do you frame a story so that people are going to read it? Probably the most widely read historian of the last three or four decades in the United States is Barbara Tuchman, who spent some seven years as a journalist before she started writing history and who did pay a great deal of attention to how she told the story, how she framed the story. And she succeeded in finding an audience, finding in fact a very important audience. President John F. Kennedy actually credited the fact that he did not declare war on the Soviet Union in 1962 over the Cuban missile crisis to the fact that he had just finished reading Barbara Tuchman's book, "*The Guns of August*," about the outbreak of World War I, and realized how easy it was to go down that slippery slope of great powers going to war when, in some sense, neither of them wanted it.

04 What was Tuchman's connection to the Cuban missile crisis?

① Tuchman was the only adviser that Kennedy would listen to during the situation.

② Tuchman's words persuaded Kennedy not to go to war with the Soviet Union.

③ Tuchman spent time explaining possible outcomes to Kennedy.

④ Tuchman decided to chronicle Kennedy's frame of mind throughout the crisis.

05 Which of the following is true, according to the passage?

① Barbara Tuchman was not accomplished at writing, but knew her facts.

② Historians can learn from journalists about how to make facts interesting.

③ Tuchman wrote her book about the Cuban missile crisis in order to help.

④ Tuchman's career as a journalist impeded her progress as a historian.

06-07

An airline loses two suitcases belonging to two different travelers. Both suitcases happen to be identical and contain identical items. An airline manager tasked to settle the claims of both travelers explains that the airline is liable for a maximum of $100 per suitcase (he is unable to find out directly the price of the items), and in order to determine an honest appraised value of the antiques the manager separates both travelers so they can't confer, and asks them to write down the amount of their value at no less than $2 and no larger than $100. He also tells them that if both write down the same number, he will treat that number as the true dollar value of both suitcases and reimburse both travelers that amount. However, if one writes down a smaller number than the other, this smaller number will be taken as the true dollar value, and both travelers will receive that amount along with a bonus/malus : $2 extra will be paid to the traveler who wrote down the lower value and a $2 deduction will be taken from the person who wrote down the higher amount. The challenge is : what strategy should both travelers follow to decide the value they should write down?

06 Why does the airline manager separate the two travelers?

① In order to encourage each traveler to be more honest.

② So that they can't talk together to decide how they should best proceed.

③ To make sure they did not try to escape together.

④ So they would have more freedom to think clearly about the value.

07 Choose the correct statement from the following.

① The traveler who writes down a higher number than the other will receive nothing.

② If both travelers put forward the same number, they will not receive any reimbursement.

③ The range within which the total value could be covered 100 dollars.

④ If one traveler writes down a smaller number, he will receive some additional benefit.

08–11

Thanks to in vitro fertilization (IVF), the skyrocketing use of fertility drugs and the increasing number of women who delay childbearing until their 30s or 40s, the incidences of multiple births have increased in the past two decades. In 1980, IVF — in which hormones are used to induce the production of eggs, which are externally fertilized and then implanted back into the uterus — became available in the U.S. Since then, the percentage of twins and triplets as a proportion of total births has increased several-fold. It's almost as if no one is impressed by them anymore. Multiple births have become easier, yet the dangers are very real for both mothers and children alike.

Multiples, as opposed to singletons, are more likely to be born premature (the more fetuses, the earlier labor occurs). The risk of miscarriage is higher. Cesarean sections are utilized more frequently. Gestational diabetes, hypertension and preeclampsia can all occur. Multiple births can also create potential long-term health implications for the children, like cerebral palsy. In the short term, in many multiple-birth situations, newborns are at greater risk of birth complications and death, though notably, all eight of the kids born to "Octomom" Nadya Suleman earlier in 2009 survived.

08 Which of the following can be inferred?

① Nadya Suleman must have done research on how to care for herself during pregnancy.

② Multiple births are still extremely rare although becoming more common.

③ Multiple births are fraught with problems for both mother and child.

④ Some women pursue IVF in order to have a greater chance of multiple births.

09 Which of the following cannot be blamed as a contributor to more multiple births?

① The fast increase in medicine used to increase fertility.

② The effects of in vitro fertilization on a woman

③ The postponement of pregnancy by women until later on in life

④ The lifestyles that modern women experience.

10 How does IVF work?

① The woman is injected with hormones that are essential for encouraging safe conception in the uterus.

② Medicine is used to alter the egg production rate which in turn means that the uterus becomes more efficient at hosting a baby.

③ Hormonally-strong eggs are produced which can then be taken out of the woman to develop in a lab.

④ Egg production is stimulated, of which some are removed and fertilized and then put back into the woman.

11 Which of the following is true?

① It is more likely that a woman will lose the babies before giving birth in a singleton birth instead of a multiple birth.

② The woman who gave birth to eight babies was already aware that some of her babies had developmental problems.

③ The complications in multiple births discouraged a woman from giving birth to all eight of her babies.

④ Despite the risks, one woman was able to carry eight babies to term and they lived.

12–14

Speaking of the perceived need for crisis, let's talk about the "burning platform," a familiar phrase in the organizational change literature. It refers to a horrific accident that happened in 1988 on the Piper Alpha oil platform in the North Sea. A gas leak triggered an explosion that ripped the rig in two. As a reporter wrote, "Those who survived had a nightmarish choice: to jump as far as 150 ft. down into a fiery sea or face certain death on the disintegrating rig." Andy Mochan, a superintendent on the rig, said, "It was fry or jump, so I jumped." He was eventually saved by a rescue mission involving NATO and the Royal Air Force.
Out of this human tragedy has emerged a rather ridiculous business cliche. When executives talk about the need for a "burning platform," they mean, basically, that they need a way to scare their employees into changing. To create a burning platform is to paint such a gloomy picture of the current state of things that employees can't help but jump into the fiery sea. (And by "jump into the fiery sea," what we mean is that they change their organizational practices. Which suggests that this use of "burning platform" might well be the dictionary definition of hyperbole.) In short, the "burning platform" is a great, uplifting tale for your people: "Team, let's choose a dangerous plunge into the ocean over getting burned to death! Now get back to work!"

12 What is the passage mainly about?

① A tragedy that changed the face of business.
② The origins of the phrase "burning platform"
③ Making decisions under extreme pressure
④ Changing safety practices to provide better protection.

13 Which of the following means the same as the underlined?

① I leaped when I was told to leap or I would not be here today.
② I chose to take a chance when my choice was either death or taking a leap into the unknown.
③ The decision I took would determine my future, and I didn't have the presence of mind at that time.
④ Jumping was not something I had ever thought I would do until that moment arrived.

14 What is the use of the phrase "burning platform" in business terms?

① To change the way things have traditionally been done by presenting a negative evaluation.
② To make people work harder without realizing they are doing it.
③ To force people to do something you want by presenting a unattractive alternative.
④ To create a worse working environment that will make workers fear for their jobs.

15-18

To begin with, we lecturers must ask ourselves a basic question: why am I lecturing? What will I be able to get across to learners through a lecture that they could not get just as well and with less inconvenience by reading a book or working through an online learning module? The answer, in part, must be that the physical presence of the lecturer and the unfolding of the lecture in real time will make a difference for learners. Great lecturers not only inform learners, they also engage their imaginations and inspire them.

The core purpose of a great lecturer is not primarily to transmit information. To this end, other techniques, such as assigning a reading in a textbook or distributing an electronic copy of the notes, can be equally effective. The real purpose of a lecture is to show the mind and heart of the lecturer at work, and to engage the minds and hearts of learners. Is the lecturer enthusiastic about the topic? Why? Could I get enthused about this, too?

A great lecturer's benefit to learners extends far beyond preparing for an exam, earning a good grade, or attaining some form of professional certification. The great lecture opens learners' eyes to new questions, connections, and perspectives that they have not considered before, illuminating new possibilities for how to work and live. Without question, it also helps learners who pay attention earn a better grade, but it manages to make the topic take on a life of its own and seem worth knowing for its own sake, beyond such narrow, utilitarian advantage.

15 **How is attending a lecture different from reading a book?**

① You can listen to the enthusiasm of the lecturer and discover if you feel the same way about the topic.
② Knowing how a lecturer truly feels about a topic can change the minds of the learners.
③ When a lecturer pays attention to the learners, they feel the full benefit of the lecture.
④ Being in the same room as a great lecturer can motivate you to read more books on the subject.

16 **Which of the following paraphrases the underlined?**

① A lecturer must help learners to solve those questions they have difficulty with.
② Learners who concentrate will certainly improve their grades
③ If learners don't ask the right questions, the lecturer's attention will be directed elsewhere.
④ The questions asked by learners will bring better grades.

17 **What can be inferred from the passage?**

① Lecturers and learners need to like each other personally in order to have a symbiotic relationship.
② The writer truly believes that he/she is a great lecturer.
③ Demonstrating feeling beyond the textbook stimulates a lecture.
④ Lecturers should pool their resources to help each other to improve their lecturing skills.

18 **Which of the following is true?**

① A lecture should consistently stick to the textbook.
② Lectures should focus on transmitting information.
③ Lecturers cannot improve grades.
④ The writer himself is a lecturer.

19-20

In a poll carried out by critics, Felix Mendelssohn has been crowned the greatest child prodigy. Perhaps surprisingly, Mozart failed to make the critics' top 10. Two main factors decided who went in — our own assessment of the quality and quantity of the music they wrote at that age, and some strongly put arguments by our leading writers. Putting together a top 10 of the best composers under the age of 18 was a revealing experience. As the writer Goethe himself said nearly 200 years ago, comparing the music that Mozart was writing as a child to Mendelssohn's at the same age is like comparing "the prattle of a child" to "the cultivated talk of a grown-up person."

19 Which is a reason Mozart was not chosen?

① Mozart did not produce much work before the age of 18.

② The work he produced in his youth was far inferior to that of Mendelssohn.

③ The list compiler does not like Mozart's music.

④ It was felt that the inclusion of Mozart was not fair on the other composers.

20 Which of the following best paraphrases what Goethe said?

① The refinement of Mendelssohn's work made Mozart's look unsophisticated.

② In adulthood, Mozart produced work as good as Mendelssohn's youthful work.

③ Mozart wrote endless amounts of high quality music, but Mendelssohn wrote much fewer.

④ Mozart was childlike in his love for music, whereas Mendelssohn held himself like an adult.

07 Practice Test

Read the following passages and answer the questions. [01~20] (제한 시간: 30분)

01–02

Both book and newspaper are confessional in character, creating the effect of inside story by their mere form, regardless of content. [1] As the book page yields the inside story of the author's mental adventures, so the press page yields the inside story of the community in action and interaction. [2] Real news is bad news — bad news about somebody, or bad news for somebody. [3] In 1962, when Minneapolis had been for months (　　　　A　　　　), the chief of police said: "Sure, I miss the news, but so far as my job goes I hope the papers never come back. There is less crime around without a newspaper to pass around the ideas." [4]

01 From the context, which of the following best fits into (A)?

① without a newspaper
② with no results
③ without problems
④ to review newspaper articles

02 Which is the best place for the following sentence?

> It is for this reason that the press seems to be performing its function most when revealing the seamy side.

① [1]
② [2]
③ [3]
④ [4]

03-05

Part of Galileo's genius was to transfer the spirit of the Italian Renaissance in the plastic arts to the mathematical and observational ones. He took the competitive, empirical drive with which Florentine painters had been looking at the world and used it to look at the night sky. <u>The intellectual practices of doubting authority and trying out experiments happened on lutes and with tempera on gesso before they turned toward the stars</u>. You had only to study the previous two centuries of Florentine drawing, from the rocky pillars of Masaccio to the twisting perfection of Michelangelo, to see how knowledge grew through a contest in observation. As the physicist and historian of science Mark Peterson points out, the young Galileo used his newly acquired skills as a geometer to lecture on the architecture of Hell as Dante had imagined it, grasping the hidden truth of "scaling up": an Inferno that big couldn't be built on classical engineering principles. But the painters and poets could look at the world, safely, through the lens of religious subjects; Galileo, ______________________________, saw the religious non-subject. They looked at people and saw angels; he looked at the heavens, and didn't.

03 **How does the writer see Galileo?**

① As a intellect who saw science in a new way.

② As a fool who thought science could rival the arts.

③ As a man of kindness but no great wisdom.

④ As a smart man who used his brains in the wrong way.

04 Which of the following fits the blank best?

① looking through his lens

② as if he had not any lens

③ regardless of lens

④ through the lens of artistic ones

05 Which of the following paraphrases the underlined?

① Experiments that cast doubts on the intellect of authority figure can be made by music, art or even science.

② Only intelligent people could challenge authority with their talents.

③ Music and art encouraged scientists to do new experiments against authority.

④ Authority was challenged first by those engaged in music and art before science.

06-09

Ready or not, English is now the global language of business. More and more multinational companies are mandating English as the common corporate language — Airbus, Daimler-Chrysler, Nokia, Renault, Samsung, and Microsoft in Beijing, to name a few — in an attempt to facilitate communication and performance across geographically diverse functions and business endeavors. Adopting a common mode of speech isn't just a good idea; it's a must, even for an American company with operations overseas, for instance, or a French company focused on domestic customers. Imagine that a group of salespeople from a company's Paris headquarters get together for a meeting. Why would you care whether they all could speak English? Now consider that the same group goes on a sales call to a company also based in Paris, not realizing that the potential customer would be bringing in employees from other locations who didn't speak French. This happened at one company I worked with. Sitting together in Paris, employees of those two French companies couldn't close a deal because the people in the room couldn't communicate. It was a shocking wake-up call, and the company soon adopted an English corporate language strategy. Adopting a global language policy is not easy, and companies invariably stumble along the way. It's radical, and it's almost certain to meet with staunch resistance from employees. Many may feel at a disadvantage if their English isn't as good as others', team dynamics and performance can suffer, and national pride can get in the way. But to survive and thrive in a global economy, companies must overcome language barriers — and English will almost always be the common ground, at least for now.

06 **What is the main idea of the passage?**

① The resistance to the spread of English around the world.
② The necessity for a common global language of business.
③ The speed at which English has been accepted by others.
④ The effect on businesses of the use of English.

07 **Which of the following is NOT a reason why employees resist the change to English?**

① Employees feel under pressure to perform whenever people from the Head Office visit.

② The relationships between team members can suffer as they try to communicate in a different language.

③ Some employees feel that putting aside their own language hurts it and makes it seem less important.

④ All employees have different levels of English; those with poor English may feel inferior or be treated as such.

08 **Why is English important for global business?**

① Without knowledge of English, global businesses would be stifled as they do not understand Western culture.

② Most of the big companies originated in English-speaking countries, so it is the most convenient language.

③ Because it is easier to learn English than many of the other languages that are spoken by a large number of people.

④ In order for companies from various nations around the world to broker deals using a common language.

09 **What can be inferred from the passage?**

① France is the last European country not to have employed English as the global language of business.

② Not everyone is overjoyed at the prospect of English becoming the global language of business.

③ Americans are more successful in business because they already know English.

④ Many large global companies are resisting the emergence of English as the business language.

10-13

A vegetative state is when a person is awake but showing no signs of awareness. On recovery from the coma state, VS/UWS is characterised by the return of arousal without signs of awareness. In contrast, a coma is a state that lacks both awareness and wakefulness. Absence of awareness can only be inferred by lack of responsiveness to the environment and not as lack of consciousness that we may not be able to detect by behavioural measures. For this reason, many authors have suggested that the term 'Unresponsive Wakefulness Syndrome' (UWS) or 'post-coma unresponsiveness' (NHMRC, 2004) are more accurate descriptive terms for VS.
A person in a vegetative state may open their eyes, wake up and fall asleep at regular intervals and have basic reflexes, such as blinking when they're startled by a loud noise, or withdrawing their hand when it's squeezed hard. They're also able to regulate their heartbeat and breathing without assistance. However, a person in a vegetative state doesn't show any meaningful responses, such as following an object with their eyes or responding to voices. They also show no signs of experiencing emotions nor of cognitive function.
VS/UWS patients' eyes might be in a relatively fixed position, may track moving objects (visual pursuit), or move in a completely unsynchronised manner. Sleep-wake cycles may resume or patients may appear to be in a state of chronic wakefulness. They may grind their teeth, swallow, smile, shed tears, grunt, moan, or scream without any apparent external stimulus. VS/UWS patients do not respond to sound, hunger, or pain. Patients cannot obey verbal commands and lack local motor responses. Additionally VS/UWS patients cannot talk in comprehensible terms and may become noisy, restless, and hypermobile. One of the most challenging tasks facing clinicians is that of differentiating VS/UWS from minimally conscious (MCS) states.
Whilst neuroimaging such as MRI is widely used in assessing brain damage and functional abilities, behavioural assessment has, until now, been the "gold standard" for detecting signs of consciousness and thereby for determining diagnosis. If a person is in a vegetative state for a long time, it may be considered to be: 1) a continuing vegetative state – when it's been longer than four weeks, 2) a permanent vegetative state – when it's been more than six months if caused by a non-traumatic brain injury, or more than 12 months if caused by a traumatic brain injury. If a person is diagnosed as being in a permanent vegetative state, ________________.

10 What is the passage mainly about?

① The difficulties faced by medical professionals when dealing with VS/UWS.
② The varying characteristics associated with VS/UWS patients.
③ The best ways to overcome the limitations of being in a VS/UWS state.
④ The possibilities of recovery or not when someone enters a VS/UWS state.

11 According to the passage, which of the following is incorrect?

① When in a vegetative state, emotions and cognitive function are absent.
② A patient in a vegetative state appears to be responsive because some of it is meaningful.
③ There is no rule to how the eyes of VS/UWS patients may move or indeed not move.
④ The functioning of the heart and the lungs without assistance is seen in vegetative state patients.

12 How do doctors make a diagnosis of VS/UWS?

① They use a combination of MRI and behavioral assessment.
② They check for how long the patient has been unresponsive.
③ They talk to the patient and determine the cause of the problem.
④ They check for and rule out other similar diagnoses first.

13 Which best completes the sentence?

① the patients' loved ones usually lose all hope
② recovery is extremely unlikely but not impossible
③ doctors immediately try to do more research
④ they can understand everything going on around them

14-16

Social scientists first became aware of its effectiveness in the mid-1960s when psychologists Jonathan Freedman and Scott Fraser published an astonishing set of data. They reported the results of an experiment in which a researcher, posing as a volunteer worker, had gone door to door in a residential California neigh- borhood making a preposterous request of homeowners. The homeowners were asked to allow a public-service billboard to be installed on their front lawns. To get an idea of how the sign would look, they were shown a photograph depicting an attractive house, the view of which was almost completely obscured by a very large, poorly lettered sign reading DRIVE CAREFULLY. Although the request was normally and understandably refused by the great majority (83 percent) of the other residents in the area, this particular group of people reacted quite favorably. A full 76 percent of them offered the use of their front yards.

The prime reason for their startling compliance has to do with something that had happened to them about two weeks earlier: They had made a small commitment to driver safety. A different volunteer worker had come to their doors and asked them to accept and display a little three-inch-square sign that read BE A SAFE DRIVER. It was such a trifling request that nearly all of them had agreed to it. But the effects of that request were enormous. Because they had innocently complied with a trivial safe-driving request a couple of weeks before, these homeowners became remarkably willing to comply with another request that was massive in size.

14 What is the topic of the passage?

① Teaching society to be more compliant to the requests of others
② Using the foot in the door technique to gain compliance
③ Performing experiments in the name of furthering science
④ How social science has opened doors on to human behavior.

15 Which of the following means the same thing as the underlined?

① People consented to it because it felt like they were not being asked to do much.
② The little sign was replaced by a much larger sign when the homeowners requested.
③ Asking others to drive safely is something that everyone agrees is right.
④ Agreeing to one small thing does not mean that you agree to a much larger request.

16 Where might this passage appear?

① A pamphlet on protecting oneself from being taken advantage of
② An article on corrupt advertising companies
③ A research paper on selling tactics
④ A study on human behavior

17-20

The wisest of <u>the apostles of new educational technologies</u> recognize the power of the lecture. Randy Pausch, professor of computer science, human-computer interaction, and design at Carnegie-Mellon University made perhaps his greatest educational contribution not through a new computer interface but through his famous last lecture, delivered in 2007. Though dying of pancreatic cancer, Pausch's presentation on "Really Achieving Your Childhood Dreams" showed a lecturer on fire with ideas and brimming over with an infectious enthusiasm for discovery and for life.

Steve Jobs' 2005 commencement address at Stanford University embodied a similar spirit. In it, Jobs tells three stories, one about dropping out of Reed College after 6 months, the second about his firing by the board of directors at Apple, and the third about being diagnosed with pancreatic cancer. Each is a story about loss, even failure. Yet over the course of his presentation, Jobs conveys the powerful message that his successes were born from his failures and wouldn't have been possible without them. Ultimately, his message is about courage, the courage to follow your heart.

Pausch and Jobs could have confined their presentations to small groups, relying on much more direct interaction with a few audience members. They could have embedded their messages in interactive computer software programs that asked learners numerous questions and provided constructive feedback on their responses. They could have phoned their lectures in, using the latest distance-learning technology. Fortunately, however, they did not. Pausch and Jobs are great lecturers, not because they convey information with maximal efficiency, but because they get us thinking about our lives from fruitful new perspectives and help us to seek out and find new meaning in the work we do every day.

17 What is the main idea of the passage?

① Overcoming adversities in your life in order to succeed on a grand scale.
② The reasons why Pausch and Jobs are better than professional lecturers.
③ It doesn't matter what the topic of your lecture is as long as you know your stuff.
④ Lecture should combine information with more meaningful stories to motivate.

18 What does the underlined refer to?

① Those who devotedly buy everything that tech companies provide
② Those who have received their education through benefitting from new technology
③ Those lecturers who do not rely on technology to teach
④ Those at the forefront of technological innovation

19 What is the purpose of the third paragraph?

① To cast Pausch and Jobs as normal people who face the same trials and tribulations in life as anyone else.
② To praise Pausch and Jobs for stepping out of their comfort zones and attempting something from which most people shy away.
③ To show that even men whose lives are enmeshed in technology realize the importance of direct interaction.
④ To prove that you don't have to be as charismatic or as knowledgeable as Pausch or Jobs to give a great lecture.

20 Which of the following is correct, according to the passage?

① Jobs delivered the graduation speech for the graduates of Stanford University.
② Both Pausch and Jobs suffered from cancer, though not the same kind.
③ Jobs did not overcome all the failures he talked about, but he did overcome the important ones.
④ Pausch spoke in contrast to Jobs by focusing on educating his listeners with information.

08 Practice Test

Read the following passages and answer the questions. **[01~20]** (제한 시간: 30분)

01-03

Geneticist Richard Cawthon and colleagues at the University of Utah found shorter telomeres are associated with shorter lives. Among people older than 60, those with shorter telomeres were three times more likely to die from heart disease and eight times more likely to die from infectious disease. While telomere shortening has been linked to the aging process, it is not yet known whether shorter telomeres are just a sign of aging — like gray hair — or actually contribute to aging.

If telomerase makes cancer cells immortal, could it prevent normal cells from aging? Could we extend lifespan by preserving or restoring the length of telomeres with telomerase? If so, does that raise a risk the telomerase also will cause cancer? Scientists are not yet sure. But they have been able to use telomerase to make human cells keep dividing far beyond their normal limit in laboratory experiments, and the cells do not become cancerous.

If telomerase could be used routinely to "immortalize" human cells, it would be theoretically possible to mass produce any human cell for transplantation, including insulin-producing cells to cure diabetes patients, muscle cells for muscular dystrophy, cartilage cells for people with certain kinds of arthritis, and skin cells for people with severe burns and wounds. <u>Efforts to test new drugs and gene therapies also would be helped by an unlimited supply of normal human cells grown in the laboratory</u>.

01 **What is the significance of the discovery of the effects of telomerase?**

① It could prove to be the final cure for cancer that geneticists have been waiting for.

② It could turn out to be the ingredient for an elixir of youth.

③ It could mean that funding for its production would skyrocket.

④ It could be used to create an unlimited amount of human cells to help other diseases.

02 **Which of the following is true from the passage?**

① Supplying people with more telomerase would slow down the ageing process indefinitely.

② Scientists are being cautious in their statements and are not jumping to conclusions about telomerase.

③ Attempts to mass produce human cells using telomerase have already happened.

④ Telomerase does not work faster than normal, but causes those deficient in telomerase to reach normality.

03 **What does the underlined sentence mean?**

① Try as they might, new drugs testing and gene therapies have so far proven unsuccessful even though there is a never-ending supply of human cells available.

② Human cells that are produced through telomerase have proven through new drugs experiments and gene therapies to be superior to laboratory-made cells.

③ The supply of human cells to laboratory is already unlimited, so this breakthrough will have little effect on new drugs testing and gene therapies.

④ New drug testing and gene therapies have been hampered due to a limited supply of human cells to experiment on.

04-05

Another danger lies in the doctrine, which seems to have more currency than it deserves, that the study of literature is a discipline with the single end of making readers able to judge what is good and bad in it. This sounds austere and high-minded, but it too should be regarded with suspicion, because it means that, if anyone studies books in this spirit, he is so busy judging that he has little time or capacity to understand and absorb, to make his reading part of himself and to shape his life by it. Judgment is one thing, and imaginative experience is another, and it is too easy ______________________________. Nor is this kind of judgment usually worth having. It is in the end highly subjective, the reflection of a single man's tastes and whims, uncorrected and unguided by the humility which is necessary to any true understanding of a work of art.

04 **Which of the following best completes the blank?**

① to separate the first from the second
② to sacrifice the second to the first
③ to link the first with the second
④ to sacrifice the first to the second

05 **What is the main topic of the passage?**

① The proper judgment of writing
② How to self-reflect through literature
③ The shaping of the human
④ The study of literature

06–07

The issue of how differences in intelligence come about between individuals and groups is a topic of controversy. In the late 1800's, as Darwinism took off, the role of genetically determined capability was considered very important. In contrast, in the 1960's, views were more in favor of a "blank state" view of human intelligence — in other words, all people are capable of much more, if given conducive environmental conditions in which to reach their potential. Currently both genetics and environment are seen as playing important roles. ________________, the modern view about genetics vs environment in intelligence is "interactionism".

06 Which of the following correctly fits the blank?

① Without any doubt
② To make a long story short
③ To be more precise
④ Broadly speaking

07 Which of the following is correct, according to the passage?

① In the 1960s arose the general opinion that families offered the key to somebody's intelligence.
② These days, the idea that was prevalent in genetics in the late 1800s has come back into fashion.
③ A few decades ago, it was thought that people are born with a set future in intelligence that could not be changed.
④ Darwinism brought the issue of genetics and intelligence to the forefront of discussion.

08-10

We must therefore look at ________________________________, and consider our scholar as man in the abstract, man exposed to all the changes and chances of mortal life. If men were born attached to the soil of our country, if one season lasted all the year round, if every man's fortune were so firmly grasped that he could never lose it, then the established method of education would have certain advantages; the child brought up to his own calling would never leave it, he could never have to face the difficulties of any other condition. But when we consider the fleeting nature of human affairs, the restless and uneasy spirit of our times, when every generation overturns the work of its predecessor, can we conceive a more senseless plan than to educate a child as if he would never leave his room, as if he would always have his servants about him? If the wretched creature takes a single step up or down he is lost. This is not teaching him to bear pain; it is training him to feel it.

08 **What is the idea of the passage?**

① Human affairs are unforeseeable, so our education must fill in the blanks of our future.

② Education must be varied as to equip one with knowledge to face anything that may be thrown at him.

③ Each new generation must be educated not to make the same mistakes that its predecessor did.

④ If a child is not educated, he has had his future stolen from him.

09 Which of the following best resembles the underlined?

① A child who is conceived by somebody with no idea about education will fail in life.

② Deciding on a plan for education must involve consideration of the child's future.

③ It is nonsensical not to educate a child to face the challenges of the outside world.

④ A child who is educated only on what he will experience is not educated at all.

10 Choose the one that best fills in the blank.

① the general as well as the particular

② not so much the general as the particular

③ the general rather than the particular

④ either the general or the particular depending on the situation

11-13

Numerous home remedies for hiccups exist. The reason that these remedies are thought to work is that carbon dioxide build-up in the blood will stop hiccups, which is what happens when a person holds their breath. If the vagus nerve that runs from the brain to the stomach is stimulated, hiccups can also be alleviated (this is what is happening when a person drinks water or pulls on their tongue).

Try these methods at home to get rid of the hiccups: 1) Hold your breath. 2) Drink a glass of water quickly. 3) Have someone frighten you (or better, surprise) the person 4) Use smelling salts. 5) Have the person pull hard on their tongue. 6) Place one-half teaspoon of dry sugar on the back of the tongue. (Repeat this process 3 times at 2-minute intervals, if necessary use corn syrup, not sugar, in young children.)

There are many other suggestions such as “name 10 famous men” (this distracts the person with the hiccups and may help the diaphragm relax), “a finger in the ear,” tickling the palate with a swab, swallowing a tablespoon full of honey, but a person should only try those methods they feel comfortable with and be aware that some are not suitable for infants (honey, sugar methods), elderly with swallowing problems and others with health problems. Call the doctor for further information if individuals have any questions about home remedies or if they fail to stop the hiccups.

11 What is the tone of the passage?

① Humorous stories about different strange methods of curing hiccups
② Old wives' tales passed down from generation to generation.
③ Useless advice that the writer has heard over the years to cure hiccups.
④ Professional medical advice about how to cure hiccups

12 Which out of the following groups of people can follow the advice above?

① Very young children
② Senior citizens with swallowing difficulties
③ Anyone with health issues
④ Pregnant women

13 All of the following are false, except ______________________.

① drinking water provides no known assistance to hiccups
② distracting the attention of somebody causes the diaphragm to loosen up
③ raising the levels of carbon dioxide in the blood helps to get rid of hiccups
④ sniffing smelling salts will jolt your system and maybe stop the hiccups

14–16

Beauty, I have already said, is generally and most simply defined as that which gives pleasure; and thus people are driven into admitting that eating and smelling and other physical sensations can be regarded as arts. It has now been superseded in the main by a theory of aesthetics derived from Benedetto Croce, and though Croce's theory has met with a flood of criticism, its general tenet, that art is perfectly defined when simply defined as intuition, has proved to be much more illuminating than ____________________. The difficulty has been to apply a theory depending on such vague terms as 'intuition' and 'lyricism'. But the point to note immediately is, that this elaborate and inclusive theory of the arts gets on very well without the word 'beauty'.

14 **What is the opinion on Croce's theory of aesthetics?**

① It is not a perfect theory since it is so vague and it has faced much criticism, yet it is the best theory there has so far been.

② The amount of criticism that has as yet been directed at this theory means that it cannot possibly be taken seriously.

③ It shines a light on just how difficult it is to expound theories of aesthetics these days when people are so ready to criticize.

④ It talks to our basic instincts of aesthetics, but that is not enough for its critics who think Croce's theory is insufficient.

15 **Which of the following is correct, according to the passage?**

① A theory that is based on intuition has an extremely limited and narrow field of vision.

② Using intuition to support a theory means that nobody can say it is totally wrong.

③ Beauty is not only used to describe pleasurable things but also non-pleasurable things.

④ It is possible to describe things experienced though our human senses as a work of art.

16 **Choose the one that best fills in the blank.**

① the newest concept

② any previous theory

③ all the contradictory ideas

④ any dogmatic theory

17-20

The electric clocks in my house keep better time than the ones I wind, yet I scarcely look at them. It is the ticking, I think, that comforts me. I like to lean my ear against these various pendulums and, back and forth, gently rock my life away. These ticks and tocks give me a meter to the passage of the day; they are a metaphor for silence. Silence, after all, is not an absence of noise but a subtle acknowledgment of this metronomic beat, the force that both brings new life and inscribes tomorrow's obituaries. There is luxury and terror in this act of resignation, this silent attention to the ticking of our lives.

Silence's most eloquent contradiction is music — not because music breaks silence with its sounds but because it interrupts its motion. All the arts do this: books freeze events between two covers, pictures pin them against a wall. But music goes viscerally to the source of our mortality. It stops time in its tracks and reinvents it. What a supernatural act it is to command a tempo and a rhythm, to set time in motion and bring it to a halt. In a life of temporal endlessness, the musician who makes time start and stop plays at being God. This is music's comfort and its triumph: that somewhere there exists an antidote for decay.

Music scarcely exists any more, having multiplied itself into silence. This probably makes no sense at all to you, but let me try to explain. To call music an interruption is also to say it is an event, something that can seize our attention only if it is preceded by uneventfulness, and then succeeded by it. When I first heard Bach's B-minor Mass some 35 years ago, that's how I experienced it — like a monolith rising out of an empty plain, a magisterial presence defined by the emptiness around it.

17 **Which is the best title for the passage?**

① Music is the Devil
② Silence is Golden
③ A New and Awful Silence
④ The Emptiness of Music

18 **Why are musicians likened to God?**

① Nobody else, but musicians and God, can control time.
② Musicians are worshipped in a God-like way.
③ Musicians learned from God how to move people.
④ Both are thought to have a ghostly influence on people.

19 **Which of the following is true, according to the passage?**

① Silence means that nothing can be heard.
② Pieces of art have the power to disrupt time.
③ Musicians can rightly be called musicians.
④ Music can solve a multitude of life's problems.

20 **What's the most likely topic for the next part of the passage?**

① An analysis of the type of modern music that even somebody like Bach would be proud to have composed.
② A comparison between the music that greatly influenced the writer 35 years ago, and the music that doesn't affect him now.
③ An explanation of why the writer thinks that music is gradually deteriorating and will finally disappear.
④ A review of the most influential music that has ever been written.

09 Practice Test

Read the following passages and answer the questions. **[01~20]** (제한 시간 : 30분)

01-02

Think of a medical student attending a course in the X-ray diagnosis of pulmonary diseases. He watches, in a darkened room, shadowy traces on a fluorescent screen placed against a patient's chest, and hears the radiologist commenting to his assistants, in technical language, on the significant features of these shadows. At first, the student is completely puzzled. For he can see in the X-ray picture of a chest only the shadows of the heart and ribs with a few spidery blotches between them. The experts seem to be romancing about figments of their imagination; he can see nothing that they are talking about. Then, as he goes on listening for a few weeks, looking carefully at ever-new pictures of different cases, a tentative understanding will dawn on him; he will gradually forget about the ribs and begin to see the lungs. And eventually, if he perseveres intelligently, a rich panorama of significant details will be revealed to him; of physiological variations and pathological changes, of scars, of chronic infections and signs of acute disease. He has entered a new world. He still sees only a fraction of what the experts can see, but the pictures are definitely making sense now and so do most of the comments made on them.

01 **What can be inferred from the passage?**

① Not all medical students will be able to understand radiology, but the best will excel in it.
② The world of radiology is one that takes a long time and a lot of experience to understand.
③ It is common for radiologists to get exasperated with medical students who can't see what they see.
④ The technical language used by radiologists is quite unlike any other and alienates many students.

02 **Why can medical students not see anything the radiologist is referring to at first?**

① They are only seeing the most prominent features of the X-ray and not looking beyond that.
② They cannot distinguish between what is bone and what is muscle and tissue.
③ They find the technical part of X-rays boring as they want to do something more exciting.
④ They have very little training in X-rays while in medical school, which hampers their understanding.

03-04

Evidence of morality has been observed in animal behaviour studies. Stories of animals feeding disabled ones are remarkably common. Morality seems to have evolved from play. Morality is like a game with rules, and punishments for breaking them. Animals play out of choice, and continued participation depends upon empathy, fairness, co-operation and trust. Animals that habitually cheat don't get played with. Through it, each animal gets to understand what is acceptable to others and what is not — what is right, and what is wrong. Play, for social animals, is essential practice for sociality, and the rules of sociality for any species are its morals.

03 **What does the underlined it refer to?**

① morality gained from games
② cheating through habit
③ playing games together with others
④ acceptable behavior

04 **What cannot be inferred from the passage?**

① Animals create their own set of new rules when they play a game.
② Animals that are allowed to play games develop morality.
③ Animals that are new to games might cheat or do unacceptable things.
④ Animals that play lots of games get more social awareness.

05-06

The ancient Greeks believed that Homer's epic, *The Iliad* was something more than fiction. They thought it chronicled a real war, and reflected the authentic struggles of their ancestors. But modern scholars have generally been more skeptical. The epic describes a culture that thrived hundreds of years before Homer was born, and which would have seemed legendary even to him. Scholars have allowed that a kernel of historical truth might be tucked beneath the layers of heroic hyperbole and poetic embroidery, but only a small kernel.

05 What does the underlined phrase imply?

① It was autobiographical.
② It was non-fiction.
③ It arose from a dream.
④ It was untrue.

06 Which of the following is true?

① The events that are described in The Iliad were thought by ancient Greeks to have actually taken place.
② Scholars now believe that the events of The Iliad are complete works of fiction.
③ Homer dispensed with any factual accuracies in order to create a better work of art.
④ Ancient Greeks knew that the events were exaggerated, but didn't care.

07-10

Here is an idea. At the outset of yearly budget planning, marketers should take their marketing budget and split it 70-30. The 70% bucket can fund marketing and communications that support the rhythm of the business, the calendar of activity that is happening from the company's perspective (product launches, peak sales periods, sponsorships, etc.). The 30% bucket is set aside. It is used in a much more spontaneous manner, enabling marketers to activate their brand within social media by tapping into trending topics and connecting with consumers about the issues that matter today.

Marketers know that if you want to be successful within social media and be part of the conversation, you need to weave your brand and messages into current topics. Frustration sets in when an opportunity is right there in front of you, but there is no marketing budget available or the marketing plan is finalized and there just isn't room for new activities. Successful marketers today are flexible and fluid, aligning their brands with the lives of their consumers all 365 days ______________________.

If social media marketing is largely about being relevant and authentic, the best chance for success is to be nimble and take advantage of the opportunities that arise.

07 **What is the passage about?**

① Budgetary decisions that need to be made before marketing begins
② How successful marketers organize their budget.
③ Why budget planning is important for marketers.
④ The significance of social media on marketing

08 **What is the 30% set aside for?**

① It is for making sure that the marketing team can look better.
② It is for paying off those who try to stand in the way.
③ It can be used when the moment suddenly calls for it.
④ It is for cleaning up any mistakes that are made.

09 **Choose the phrase the fits in the blank.**

① going as far as possible
② not just during pre-defined campaigns
③ focused on their key targets
④ guarantee the best marketing

10 **What can be inferred from the passage?**

① The company doesn't care what consumers actually want, but instead cares more about what they think the consumer ought to want.
② Consumers find themselves responding to companies that seem to feel the same way they do about the important issues of today.
③ By fixing your marketing budget completely, you are doomed to failure and no amount of good ideas is going to save you.
④ Successful marketing is based much more these days on being on trend and capitalizing on the fast-paced nature of social media.

11-13

America has a competitive lead over others in the technology field as a result of its workforce being highly productive and quite well-educated. Higher education in the States is considered among the best globally and works by itself as a growth sector. Nariman Behravesh, chief economist of IHS Global Insight, says that it is often forgotten that American higher education is exported to the foreign students who flood to the country and pay full tuition fees for the privilege. As the dollar drops, it is cheaper and cheaper to study in America. For example, the fall of 2009 saw a whopping 70% of U.S. high school graduates continue into higher education; in addition, foreign students increased 11% from 2006 to 2009. The job market in the U.S. rests on getting more and more education. All rich countries are seeing that to remain competitive, they need to keep moving up in every sector. China produces pretty much everything but it does not have the innovation that creates those products, and that is where the best jobs are. ______________________________, America needs to continue creating innovative college graduates, especially in science fields, and ensure existing workers receive additional retraining to move into new job sectors. The last recession clearly showed the gap between the kind of people looking for jobs and the kind of jobs available to them. Somebody who has been trained as a machinist or builder does not have the skills necessary to get one of the many nursing or teaching jobs going. Bernard Baumohl, chief global economist for the Princeton, N.J. — based Economic Outlook Group, agrees that the economy has a glaring mismatch in jobs and workers. Those who have been out of work for over 6 months are most at risk. Having been trained in something all your life does not help you at all when you suddenly want a change of career. You have no skills or qualifications to make that change.

11 What is the best title for the passage?

① The future of U.S. exports is innovation.
② China's lack of creativity in the face of the U.S.
③ How to build and maintain better schools
④ The new future for U.S. employment

12 Which of the following best completes the sentence?

① Getting those jobs, however, is easier said than done
② In order to retain this competitive edge
③ Since America has been able to stay at the top of the table
④ When those jobs inevitably begin to dry up

13 What is the most likely topic of the next paragraph?

① How China will compete with the U.S. in the future.
② What will happen if no work force remains to maintain the U.S. jobs.
③ The next new innovation from the U.S.
④ How workers can acquire new skills in the U.S.

14–16

It is a fact that what is now the most popular word in the world — O.K. — did not come about in a serious way. It was the fashion in the late 1830s for American newspapers to use abbreviations, and in a way that was meant to be funny though doesn't appear to be so today. Metcalf spends a whole chapter discussing the amusement of Boston Morning Post readers who saw o.k. used as an abbreviation of "oll korrect", a deliberate mispelling of "all correct". The humor is lost on me. However, then, people wishing to discredit Andrew Jackson started a rumor that he could not spell and used the abbreviation "o.k." to approve papers. Metcalf acknowledges the falseness of the rumor, but the word stuck and gained traction as a real word. It began to be the phrase of choice for telephone operators to say "all clear". It traveled around the world very quickly. It has been said that technically it was the first word spoken on the moon. It was used to begin the heroic fight of Todd Beamer on 9/11. It is so normal that it needs some embellishment, such as the "okely dokely" of Ned Flanders. What is amazing about the word OK is not its popularity or its birth but ____________________. 20th century foreigners saw the word as implying "American simplicity, pragmatism, and optimism". Today, the word simply means the American concept of tolerance and respect for difference. In such unstable times, there is something comforting in the knowledge that a small two-letter word can bring people together.

14 What can be inferred from the passage?

① OK will continue to be used for a while but will eventually be replaced.
② Words like OK sometimes become part of everyday English even if that wasn't the original intention.
③ Today OK along with several other words encapsulate what it means to be American for most people.
④ OK has many different definitions and meanings associated with it that will change with time.

15 How did OK become a commonly used word according to the passage?

① Andrew Jackson used it.
② Telegraph operators started to use it.
③ Americans began to use it in everyday speech.
④ It was said by Todd Beamer.

16 Which of the following best completes the sentence?

① its symbolism of an American way of thinking
② how many people use it without thinking
③ what the various meanings it has for so many people
④ the thought that it came out of nowhere to become great

17-20

A paywall is a system that prevents Internet users from accessing webpage content without a paid subscription. There are both "hard" and "soft" paywalls in use. "Hard" paywalls allow minimal to no access to content without subscription, while "soft" paywalls allow more flexibility in what users can view without subscribing, such as selective free content and/or a limited number of articles per month, or the sampling of several pages of a book or paragraphs of an article. Newspapers have been implementing paywalls on their websites to increase their revenue, which has been diminishing due to a decline in print subscriptions and advertising revenue. While paywalls are used to bring in extra revenue for companies by charging for online content, they have also been used to increase the number of print subscribers. Some newspapers offer access to online content, including delivery of a Sunday print edition at a lower price point than online access alone. News sites such as BostonGlobe.com and NYTimes.com use this tactic because it increases both their online revenue and their print circulation (which in turn provides more ad revenue). Creating online ad revenue has been an ongoing battle for newspapers — currently an online advertisement only brings in 10-20% of the funds brought in by a duplicate print ad. It is said that "neither digital ad cash nor digital subscriptions via a paywall are in anything like the shape that will be needed for [newspapers] to take the strain if a print presence is wiped away." According to Poynter media expert Bill Mitchell, in order for a paywall to generate sustainable revenue, newspapers must create "new value" (higher quality, innovative, etc.) in their online content that merits payment which previously free content did not. Most news coverage of the use of paywalls analyzes them from the perspective of commercial success, whether through increasing revenue by growing print subscriptions or solely through paywall revenue. However, <u>as a solely profit-driven device, the use of a paywall also brings up questions of media ethics pertaining to accessible democratic news coverage</u>.

17 **What is the main idea of the passage?**

① Paywalls are used by newspapers to generate more revenue but it does not bring in as much as would be needed if the print business collapsed.
② Paywalls are being utilized by newspapers as last-ditch attempts to save their businesses that are being eaten up by online content.
③ Paywalls help nobody as they do not bring in enough profit for the newspapers to be satisfied and they are not liked by customers.
④ Paywalls are a great way for newspapers to revive their flagging fortunes but they are not marketed to consumers aggressively enough.

18 **How can newspapers increase traffic to their online sites?**

① The content must carry exclusives and be the first to report major news stories.
② The content has to be of a higher quality to warrant the subscription.
③ The subscription must be low enough to attract people.
④ Some of the content needs to be free to entice readers in to the paid content.

19 **Which of the following topics is covered in the article?**

① The resurgence of print media
② Bypassing hard and soft paywalls
③ The low revenue of online ads
④ The media ethics of total coverage

20 **Which of the following best paraphrases the underlined?**

① Since the paywall requires money to access news, the question of whether it is democratic to charge for access to news is raised.
② It is almost impossible to satisfy both the needs of a democracy and the needs of a company that exists purely to make money.
③ The ethics of using paywalls to ensure that only a limited number of readers have access to democratic content is coming to the forefront.
④ As profits become more important in the media, one wonders if it is ethical to limit access to content by means of a paywall in order to best serve the public.

10 Practice Test

Read the following passages and answer the questions. **[01~20]** (제한 시간: 30분)

01-03

Persephone is the goddess of the underworld in Greek mythology. She is the daughter of Zeus and Demeter, goddess of the harvest. Persephone was such a beautiful young woman that everyone loved her, even Hades wanted her for himself. One day, when she was collecting flowers on the plain of Enna, the earth suddenly opened and Hades rose up from the gap and abducted her. None but Zeus, and the all-seeing sun, Helios, had noticed it.

Broken-hearted, Demeter wandered the earth, looking for her daughter until Helios revealed what had happened. Demeter was so angry that she withdrew herself in loneliness, and the earth ceased to be fertile. Knowing this could not continue much longer, Zeus sent Hermes down to Hades to make him release Persephone. Hades grudgingly agreed, but before she went back he gave Persephone a pomegranate (or the seeds of a pomegranate, according to some sources). When she later ate some of it, it bound her to the underworld forever and she had to stay there one-third of the year. The other months she stayed with her mother. When Persephone was in Hades, Demeter refused to let anything grow and winter began. This myth is a symbol of the budding and dying of nature.

01 Why did Zeus realize that Persephone needed to be released?

① Hades owed Demeter a big favor and Zeus was the man to grant it.
② Demeter's anger was causing problems in Zeus' own life.
③ Hades did not wish to have Persephone by his side anymore.
④ The earth was no longer producing crops, or supporting vegetation.

02 What is the most likely message of this story?

① A warning about letting daughters walk alone
② An argument for mothers being too overbearing
③ A diatribe on the sinful actions of men
④ An explanation as to why the seasons change

03 What can be inferred about Hades?

① He did not usually desire women, especially for their beauty.
② He was known to abduct women quite frequently.
③ Whenever he wandered the woods, women were afraid.
④ He truly loved Persephone as both a sister and a friend.

04-06

Even when obese, men tend to have more muscle mass than women. Women carry approximately 10% more of their body weight in fat. Furthermore, several studies have shown that a man's metabolism is anywhere from 3% to 10% higher than a woman's of the same weight and age. That brings us to a physiological truth: the more muscle you have, the higher your metabolism will be and the more calories you will burn, even when resting.

The type of extra weight you're carrying matters too. Men tend to have more visceral fat, the kind that accumulates deep in the body, mostly around the organs in their midsections. It may not jiggle around, but it can give a guy some added girth or a big gut. Women have more subcutaneous fat, which sits just under the skin (most often in your hips and thighs). This type of fat tends to jiggle and move, and you might even (unhappily) be able to grab hold of it.

While visceral fat is the more dangerous of the two and has been linked to a long list of health issues, a 2009 study at Cairo University showed that it gets metabolized faster than subcutaneous fat. This means that subcutaneous fat is harder to lose, which is just another hurdle for women who are looking to lose weight.

04 **What is the purpose of the passage?**

① To illustrate the differences in the troubles that men and women face with their weight.

② To help women understand why they are not able to do what men are capable of.

③ To offer advice on how best to approach the issue of weight loss among the sexes.

④ To give the most informed opinion possible on the different methods of weight loss.

05 What is the benefit to being a woman compared to a man according to the passage?

① Men do not have the ability to jiggle their fat while women can.
② It is easier to see the fat that women have, and therefore they can see improvement faster.
③ A woman is less likely to suffer medically due to her fat than a comparable male.
④ A woman is able to remove the fat from her body in a healthier manner than a man is capable of.

06 What is another way of saying the same as the underlined in the passage?

① It probably doesn't move in the same way.
② It most likely remains rather stable and unmoving.
③ It looks really hard.
④ It is one big solid mass that does not move.

07-10

The verifiability criterion of meaning was essential to logical positivism. In its first and simplest form the criterion said just that the meaning of a synthetic statement is the method of its empirical verification. (Analytic statements were held to be logically verifiable.) The point of the principle was to class metaphysical statements as meaningless, since such statements (Kant's claim that noumenal matters are beyond experience was a favored example) could obviously not be empirically verified. This initial formulation of the criterion was soon seen to be too strong; it counted as meaningless not only metaphysical statements but also statements that are clearly empirically meaningful, such as that all copper conducts electricity and, indeed, any universally quantified statement of infinite scope, as well as statements that were at the time beyond the reach of experience for technical, and not conceptual, reasons, such as that there are mountains on the back side of the moon. These difficulties led to modification of the criterion: The latter to allow empirical verification if not in fact then at least in principle, the former to soften verification to empirical confirmation. So, that all copper conducts electricity can be confirmed, if not verified, by its observed instances. Observation of successive instances of copper that conduct electricity in the absence of counterinstances supports or confirms that all copper conducts electricity, and the meaning of "all copper conducts electricity" could thus be understood as the experimental method of this confirmation.

07 **What is the main idea of the passage?**

① The meaninglessness of metaphysical and empirically verified statements.

② Why analytic and synthetic statements cannot be understood as the same thing.

③ The verifiability criterion and its modification.

④ The long task of finding out whether all copper can conduct electricity or not.

08 **What is the most likely topic of the paragraph directly preceding this passage?**

① Some varied examples of empirical verification.

② The meaning of the verifiability criterion of meaning.

③ Kant's relationship in the community of logical positivists.

④ General thoughts about logical positivism.

09 **Which closely resembles the underlined sentence?**

① If we cannot verify the electrical conduction of copper, then we can surely not confirm it either.

② By observing the times when copper conducts electricity, we can confirm that it in fact does, but we cannot verify it.

③ The difference between confirmation and verification is hardly seen in the conduction of electricity by copper.

④ The instances when we actually observe copper conducting electricity cannot be confirmed or verified.

10 **Which of the following is a correct statement?**

① Both analytic and synthetic statements were rejected as meaningful by logical positivists.

② The original scope of the verifiability criterion of meaning remains unchanged since its inception.

③ Scientists were able to verify that there were mountains on the back side of the moon.

④ It is impossible to empirically state metaphysical statements with 100% certainty.

11-13

Ever wonder why women can brush their teeth while walking and talking on various subjects while men generally find this very difficult to do? Why 99 percent of all patents are registered by men? Why stressed women talk? Why so many husbands hate shopping? According to Barbara and Allan Pease, science now confirms that "the way our brains are wired and the hormones pulsing through our bodies are the two factors that largely dictate, long before we are born, how we will think and behave. Our instincts are simply our genes determining how our bodies will behave in given sets of circumstances." That's right: socialization, politics, or upbringing aside, men and women have profound brain differences and are intrinsically inclined to act in distinct — and consequently frustrating — ways.

The premises behind Why Men Don't Listen and Women Can't Read Maps is that all too often, these differences get in the way of fulfilling relationships and that understanding our basic urges can lead to greater self-awareness and ____________ ____________________________. The Peases spent three years researching their book — traveling the globe, talking to experts, and studying the cutting-edge research of ethnologists, psychologists, biologists, and neuroscientists — <u>yet their work does not read a bit like "hard science</u>." In fact, the authors go to considerable lengths to point out that their book is intended to be funny, interesting, and easy to read; in short, this is a book whose primary purpose is to talk about "average men and women, that is, how most men and women behave most of the time, in most situations, and for most of the past."

11 Which of the following most closely resembles the underlined phrase?

① however the book is not written in the style of serious scientific theories
② although the book is mean to be read by hardened scientists
③ even though the book doesn't actually contain any scientific facts
④ as if their work is written for those interested in hard science

12 What do the Peases believe?

① Men and women are essentially the same.
② Our hormones and genetics determine the way we act in the world.
③ Babies are born as blank sheets and our environment shapes us to act in certain ways.
④ Women and men both enjoy perpetuating stereotypes.

13 Which of the following best fits for the blank?

① fewer differences between men and women
② understand to speak differently
③ improved relations between the sexes
④ analyze the in the American culture

14-15

The U.S. government profits from the fact that people all over the world love our green pieces of paper. How does the government actually profit? Through something called seigniorage, which is as hard to explain as it is to spell. In the old days, seigniorage was the revenue the government earned because it costs less than a dollar to print a dollar. Say it costs 2 cents to print a $1 dollar bill. Then, poof, the government has gained something like 98 cents when it prints that dollar and uses it to buy something. That's overly simple but it's a good starting place. Today the Federal Reserve controls the money supply. And one of the ways it does this is by buying or selling treasury bills. If the Fed wants to increase the money supply, it buys some treasury bills (government bonds) from banks. So a treasury bill is taken out of circulation and replaced, basically, with dollars. Presto. More dollars in the world. Here's the key part: more dollars in circulation means more treasury bills at the Fed. And unlike dollars, the treasury bills earn interest. So the Fed profits. It's holding onto those treasury bills, which pay off with interest. Basically, when you hold onto U.S. cash, you're giving the Federal Reserve an interest-free loan.

14 What cannot be inferred from the passage?

① If the Fed is holding lots of treasury bills, there are more dollars in circulation.
② Seigniorage references when the government makes money by printing money.
③ By increasing the money in circulation, the Federal Reserve makes money.
④ Having lots of US dollars is an easy way to depreciate its value and reduce its influence.

15 What do the two words 'poof' and 'presto' imply?

① The things that happen are unfair.
② What the author is saying is true.
③ Things happen instantly, like magic.
④ Any criticism is unwarranted.

16-17

The use of symbolism to avoid censorship is as old as language itself. In the antebellum U.S., Harriet Tubman communicated with fugitives escaping slavery by singing songs with hidden meanings that their pursuers would not understand. One scholar says the cycle of code making and code breaking "_______________." In French, for instance, slang words known as verlan are created by transposing the syllables of an existing word. Because many verlan terms originated as a secret code to discuss illicit behavior, the process was often repeated when a new form became too recognizable. In this way, femme (the standard word for "woman") gave rise to meuf, which in turn became feumeu. Analogously, online coded symbols evolve as their previously secret meanings become well-known.

On the Internet, such symbols can manifest as words or visual motifs, including emoji, memes or other images. The specific form of a symbol ultimately matters less than the idea it represents, says Ryan Milner, who studies Internet culture at the College of Charleston. But he notes that visual symbols have proved particularly effective at evading censorship, thanks to their inherent ambiguity. And their power to spread rapidly online derives from their ability to establish an in-group and out-group. "As they get more esoteric, as they get more inside jokey, then there's more and more of a signal that 'if you get this, if you're part of the joke—then you are one of us,'" Milner says, "and 'if you don't get it..., then you're not one of us."

16 According to the passage, which of the following is correct?

① On the Internet, visual symbols spread quicker than words.
② Everybody knows what a particular visual symbol means when they see it.
③ It is easy to censor visual symbols on the Internet due to their clarity.
④ Those who understand coded symbols are often left out groups.

17 Which best completes the sentence?

① only works in certain communities
② is rejected by educated societies
③ is a major driver of language change
④ prevents language evolution

18–20

Since 9/11, an increasingly popular justification for limiting immigration is the need to secure the safety of one's citizens. After all, given the presence of international terrorists, one can hardly question the threat posed by at least some foreigners. No one can deny the moral importance of protecting innocent civilians from a terrorist attack, but critics have questioned whether restricting immigration is in fact likely to provide the desired security. Chandran Kukathas, for instance, raises two important concerns. First, he notes that, while laws to limit immigration may well decrease legal immigration, they will not realistically be able to eliminate all illegal immigrants. And this point is relevant, of course, because foreign terrorists who feel so passionately about their causes so as to be willing to carry out terrorist missions are not likely to be dissuaded from doing so by the illegality of entering the country whose citizens they seek to attack. Second, even if a state could somehow eliminate all legal and illegal immigration, this would not be enough because foreigners routinely enter countries, not as immigrants, but for shorter periods as tourists, guest workers, visiting students, or for short business trips. Thus, ________________ ____, it could not reasonably hope to exclude all foreign terrorists unless it also restricted the flow of temporary visitors.

18 Which of the following is true, according to the passage?

① Establishing the security of one's citizens saw no change even after 9/11 because it has always been an issue.

② When the spotlight is on immigration laws, people usually forget their own moral principles.

③ Would-be terrorists will not be deterred from entering a country because they cannot legally immigrate there.

④ 9/11 saw an increased fear amongst those wishing to immigrate to another country.

19 Which of the following fits the blank?

① if a country that has somehow managed to preclude its immigration

② even if a country somehow managed to preclude all immigration

③ in the instance whereby immigration has been precluded in a country

④ although immigration has not yet been fully precluded in a country

20 Which of the following reflects one of the opinions of Chandran Kukathas?

① It is only by eliminating all entry to a country that a terrorist attack could be prevented.

② If a nation continues to hand out tourist visas then it must be prepared for attacks made on it.

③ It is necessary to distinguish between legal and illegal immigration in order to deter terrorist attacks.

④ Most terrorists seek to enter a country illegally in order to stay under the radar of law enforcement.

11 Practice Test

Read the following passages and answer the questions. **[01~30]** (제한 시간: 45분)

01-03

These days, coffee is practically a universal part of our modern workplace condition. Many of us harbor some secret fear that the gallons of brown liquid we're slurping every day is doing us no good. We cling to scraps of evidence — like this one suggesting coffee contributes to your daily recommended fluid intake — showing that coffee in superhuman amounts is safe. And we pour ourselves another when a new study comes out implying the stuff can make us even healthier than we already are. One study, presented last week to the Society for Experimental Biology, appears to show an appreciable benefit in the muscle strength of mice who've been given caffeine. Researchers from Coventry University examined two main muscles — the diaphragm and a key leg muscle called the extensor digitorumlongus — in their test animals before and after the treatment. They noticed a strong link between caffeine intake and better muscle performance among adult mice, with a somewhat weaker relationship for elderly subjects and a small, though still measurable, effect on juvenile mice. The scientists say their findings could be significant for people heading into their golden years, as muscles tend to weaken with age — increasing the likelihood of trips, falls and other mishaps. Who wouldn't want to be able to maintain their muscle tone by sipping a cup of coffee every morning?

01 **What cannot be inferred from the passage?**

① That there are definite benefits to drinking coffee.

② Drinking coffee is detrimental to a person's health.

③ There are many benefits to coffee/caffeine that are yet to be discovered.

④ Most people would probably drink coffee if it would be beneficial to their health in later life.

02 **What is the best title for the passage?**

① The latest research to defend your caffeine addiction

② A few reasons to quit coffee

③ People still have too much coffee.

④ Why what you do now affects you later.

03 **What is the most likely reason why most people drink coffee based on the passage?**

① They drink coffee for its medical benefit.

② They drink it because they love the taste.

③ They drink it for the caffeine kick at work.

④ They drink it because they need to get their water intake.

04-06

"Language is a guide to social reality — it powerfully conditions all thinking about social problems and processes." For this reason it is argued that language that excludes females or gives unequal treatment to males and females, contributes to the perpetuation of a society in which women are regarded by many men and women as lesser beings. Such language is referred to as, "sexist" language.

The generic use of "man" and words including, "man" such as mankind and the generic use of the masculine pronouns "he", "him", "his" and "himself" to refer to both males and females are considered to be ego-inflating to boys and, <u>ego-deflating to girls as they approach adulthood</u> and therefore a reinforcement of the implication that man is the norm and women the deviation of the species.

Sexist language also contributes to ambiguity in circumstances where usage of words including 'man' and singular masculine pronouns referring to men and women is intermingled with usage referring to men only. The existence of two such alternative interpretations is seen by opponents of sexist language as discrimination in that it raises an inference that it is a privilege for women to be accepted in some instances as being within the category of "man".

04 What can you infer about sexist language in relation to women?

① Sexist language arose from some men's hatred of women.
② Women themselves perpetuate sexist language.
③ It causes a feeling of inequality and inadequacy.
④ Women are constantly receiving unequal treatment.

05 **Which of the following is true?**

① Sexist language gives women more power.

② Most people already believe that women should feel privileged to be accepted as ‘men’.

③ It is confusing when masculine pronouns are used to cover men and women and sometimes only men.

④ Only men are affected by the sexist language.

06 **Which most closely resembles the underlined phase?**

① promising to girls who can’t wait to be adults

② inspiring to adults

③ demoralizing to teenage girls

④ perplexing to girls who will be adults soon

07-10

When Americans travel abroad, they are often surprised at how well other countries do the things we used to think America does best. In fact, one reason so many American businesses still lead the world is because they benchmark the competition and emulate best practices. But suggest to an American politician that we should try to learn from other countries, and he will look at you like you are from Mars. It is somehow unpatriotic even to raise such comparisons.

Imagine if a politician were to say, "France has a better health care system than we do." I can almost guarantee that politician would suffer electoral defeat — even though the statement, in most objective respects, is true. <u>The U.S. is, for too many, the only country that matters</u>; experiences anywhere else are irrelevant. Remember, we have many members of Congress who boast they have no passport.

At a time when many trend lines in the U.S. point to relative decline in this regard, one actually brings hope: more and more young Americans go abroad for some of their education. Last year, about a quarter million studied in another country; a decade ago, the number was about half that. Value will come not just from greater global consciousness, but from the direct experience that many nations simply do many things far better than we do.

But many of our political leaders, rather than asking what we can learn from the countries that have surpassed us in various ways, choose instead to win applause with unqualified boasts of our inherent greatness. They imply that the answers to our problems are to be found not just by closing our borders to immigrants but to foreign ideas as well.

07 What's the main idea of the passage?

① American politicians need to look to other countries for ideas about how to solve their own problems.
② American politicians are thought to be xenophobic from the way they talk of other countries.
③ American politicians should travel as much as possible before being elected.
④ If more Americans traveled abroad, they would not have so many problems.

08 All of the following are true except ______________.

① there are many members of Congress who are proud of the fact that they have never been abroad
② a politician who says another country is better than America will be rejected by Americans
③ the amount of American students who spend part of their education in another country is growing
④ france's healthcare system is not better than America's: it is just different

09 What does the author imply at the beginning of the passage?

① Americans expect to see American businesses wherever they go in the world.
② America is still considered the best in many businesses.
③ Americans do not expect the experiences they have when they travel abroad.
④ American politicians need to use their travel experiences to change the minds of average Americans.

10 What can be understood from the underlined phrase?

① This is believed by some outside of the US too.
② This may be true.
③ This is not a positive thing.
④ This is not a criticism.

11-13

According to a report in *Nature*, scientists from Oregon Health & Sciences University have successfully created human embryos with genetic information from one man and two different women. <u>The ground-breaking technique is meant to prevent the passing on of deadly mitochondrial diseases from mother to child</u>. Mitochondrial diseases occur when the mitochondria — small structures within cells responsible for producing energy — fail to function as they should. The result can be debilitating diseases from cell death and whole biological system failure. Because mitochondria are essential for energy production, people who suffer from these diseases typically have problems with organs in high need of energy — such as the brain, liver, heart and more. These kinds of diseases can range anywhere from mild and non-threatening to incapacitating and fatal. If the process is implemented, three-parent IVF is ultimately meant to diminish the incidence of mitochondrial diseases to as close to zero as possible. However, while the reason for the procedure seems noble, there has already been intense debate in Britain (where similar research has been done) over whether or not such contraception methods are ethical. Many bioethicists are commenting that just because the procedure can be done, doesn't necessarily mean it should.

11 What can you infer from the ethical question brought up in the passage is?

① Whether current methods of contraception should be tampered with to make way for modern, potentially dangerous, methods.

② Whether it is right to tamper with natural two-parent reproduction just because we have found a way to do it.

③ Whether our scientists are trained well enough in the detection of such diseases that need to be treated in such an invasive way.

④ Whether the reasons that have been given for developing this technique are done are humanistic or economically driven.

12 What is the correct paraphrase for the underlined?

① Averting the spread of mitochondrial diseases by using these techniques means that mothers cannot pass onto their children.

② Mitochondrial diseases that can have a fatal effect on a child need to be treated in the mother first using modern surgery.

③ The purpose of this pioneering practice is to put a stop to the transmission of mitochondrial diseases from parent to child.

④ When the child inherits a mitochondrial disease from their parent, immediate attention is needed to avoid complications.

13 What is the result of a mitochondrial failure on the body?

① Bodily functions do not follow normal schedules.

② Vital organs begin to slow down as they cannot keep up with the body's needs.

③ Organ failure quickly results as blood circulation slows.

④ A lack of energy in the body causes harm to internal organs.

14-16

If you see an A, and it has the characteristic x, it does not follow logically from this that the next A you see will also have the characteristic x. Either it may or it may not — there may be some A's with this characteristic and some without — unless of course you make the conjunction true by definition, which is to say you stipulate that something is to count as an A only if it has the characteristic x. But in that case the statement 'All A's are x is a tautology (a tautology is a statement that says the same thing twice, but in different words, i.e. a bachelor is an unmarried man) and conveys no empirical information.
Not only does the non-tautologous conclusion that 'All A's are x' not follow from a single observation of an A, it does not follow from two such observations, nor from two thousand, nor from two billion. The best-known example that has been used in illustration of this point has to do with swans. For thousands of years before the discovery of Australia all the swans that any Westerner had ever seen had been white, and everyone seems to have taken it for granted that all swans were white — expressions like 'swan white' or 'white as a swan' were common, and the very statement 'All swans are white' had been made familiar by being used as a recurrent example in a standard textbook of logic that was in common use at the time of the Reformation and after. But when Europeans discovered Australia they encountered, for the first time, black swans. Now they could have reacted to this by saying that because these birds were black they were not swans, but a different sort of bird, and then given them another name. That would have been to empty the statement 'All swans are white' of informational content by making it true by definition. Instead they accepted that these birds were indeed swans, and that the statement 'All swans are white' was false. But what this means is that however many millions of people over however many thousands of years, and without one single exception in all that time being seen to be white, it had never followed that all swans were white. As Hume put it: 'However easy this step may seem, reason would never, to all eternity, be able to make it.' But this in turn means that unrestrictedly general statements of the form 'All A's have the characteristic x' are, of their very nature, not empirically verifiable. And the disconcerting fact is that scientific laws are characteristically statements of this kind. So their unrestricted generality makes it permanently impossible

to verify them empirically, by no matter how many observations — trillions, zillions, any number anyone cares to name. So, said Popper, from the Verification Principle it follows that scientific laws are meaningless statements, and are empty of informational content. The Verification Principle rules out all scientific laws, and therefore the whole of science.

14 **What can be said about the statement "All swans are white"?**

① It is false, and has always been false, even though there was no evidence to prove it was false.

② It used to be true, until black swans were discovered in Australia.

③ The informational content is that the color of swans is always white, regardless of where they are from.

④ Having witnessed millions and trillions of white swans, the statement could be verified as the truth.

15 **Which of the following is an example of a tautology?**

① I received a free gift on entering the competition.

② I was quick to judge the competition.

③ Many people tried to enter the competition.

④ Everyone who entered the competition received something.

16 **What cannot be inferred from the passage?**

① All scientific laws are unable to be verified empirically.

② The discovery of Australia brought with it the discovery of never-before-seen animals.

③ The evolution of swans is best seen in those that lived in Australia.

④ It was agreed by everyone in Europe that all swans were white before they went to Australia.

17-19

The tenacious wolverine, a snow-loving carnivore sometimes called the "mountain devil," could soon join the list of species threatened by climate change — a dubious distinction putting it in the ranks of the polar bear and several other animals the government says will lose crucial habitat as temperatures rise. Federal wildlife officials Friday proposed Endangered Species Act protections for the wolverine in the Lower 48 states. That's a step twice denied under the Bush administration, then delayed in 2010 when the Obama administration said other imperiled species had priority. It likely means an end to trapping the animals for their fur outside Alaska. But federal officials said they won't use the animal's status as a means to regulate greenhouse gases blamed on climate change. And other human activities — from snowmobiling and ski resorts to timber harvest and — would not be curtailed because they do not appear to be significant threats to wolverines, officials said. There are an estimated 250 to 300 wolverines in the contiguous U.S., clustered in small, isolated groups primarily in the Northern Rockies of Montana, Idaho, Wyoming and Washington. Larger populations persist in Alaska and Canada. Maxing out at 40 pounds and tough enough to stand up to grizzly bears, the animals will be no match for anticipated declines in deep mountain snows female wolverines need to establish dens and raise their young, scientists said. In some areas, such as central Idaho, suitable habitat could disappear entirely, officials said.

17 **What's the topic of the passage?**

① The relationship between government and environmentalism
② The upcoming movement to endangered status of the wolverine
③ The selfishness of humans as they encroach on animals' habitat.
④ The specific species that are under threat in the United States.

18 **Which of the following is a not a government-recognized threat to the wolverine?**

① The young wolverines are not surviving because there isn't enough snow to make their homes.
② The conditions needed for mothers to raise their offspring is disappearing.
③ The environment in which the wolverine lives is disappearing.
④ The land where wolverines roam is being taken over for human leisure activities.

19 **Which phrase in the passage means the same as "a not necessarily positive feature"?**

① a dubious distinction
② a step twice denied
③ an end to trapping
④ a means to regulate

20-23

At the Jamba Juice shop at 53rd Street and Lexington Avenue in Manhattan, along with the juice oranges and whirring blenders is another tool vital to the business: the Weather Channel. The shop's managers frequently look at the channel's Web site and plug the temperature and rain forecast into the software they use to schedule employees. "Weather has a big effect on our business," said Nicole Rosser, Jamba's New York district manager. If the mercury is going to hit 95 the next day, for instance, the software will suggest scheduling more employees based on the historic increase in store traffic in hot weather. At the 53rd Street store, Ms. Rosser said, that can mean seven employees on the busy 11－to－2 shift, rather than the typical four or five.

Such powerful scheduling software, developed by companies like Dayforce and Kronos over the last decade, has been widely adopted by retail and restaurant chains. The Kronos program that Jamba bought in 2009 breaks down schedules into 15-minute increments. So if the lunchtime rush at a particular shop slows down at 1:45, the software may suggest cutting 15 minutes from the shift of an employee normally scheduled from 9 a.m. to 2 p.m. Karen Luey, Jamba's chief financial officer, said the scheduling software "helped us take 400, 500 basis points out of our labor costs," or 4 to 5 percentage points, a savings of millions of dollars a year. At Jamba Juice, which has 770 outlets, managers used to piece together their stores' weekly schedules on an Excel spreadsheet. It took managers about two hours to slot in 25 to 30 employees, all generally part-time except for the store manager and one or two shift managers. With the Kronos software, scheduling takes just 30 minutes.

20 **What is the opinion of the writer?**

① The employees are being taken advantage of by their employer.
② The software is economically advantageous for the company.
③ The atmosphere in the store has become more competitive.
④ The employees are not being treated decently enough.

21 **How does the store save money?**

① It only opens for the busy rush hours when they make a lot of money, and close when there are slow periods.

② The employees work hard for tips and donate any money they make back to the company that treats them well.

③ They employ fewer employees in total, but ask them to work for longer hours for less money.

④ Employees are only scheduled, and paid for, the exact time to the minute for how long the busy time lasts.

22 **Which of the following can you infer from the passage?**

① Employees have reported that they are very happy with the new scheduling.

② The software has not failed yet, remaining highly accurate every day.

③ The Weather Channel was at first annoyed by this and demanded some compensation.

④ Employees do not know their exact schedule from one day to the next.

23 **Which of the following paraphrases the underlined?**

① When the software predicts a hot day, more employees are scheduled to work to accommodate the extra customers.

② More people drink juice when it is hot out, so it is important to prepare the store at the beginning of summer.

③ While hot days bring more customers into the store, the extra traffic causes problems with supplies.

④ It is well-known that lines are longer on hot days, so customers are advised to be patient with the employees.

24–26

Art restoration is related to art conservation. Restoration is a process that attempts to return the work of art to some previous state that the restorer imagines was the "original". This was commonly done in the past. However, in the late 20th century a separate concept of conservation was developed that is more concerned with preserving the work of art for the future, and less with making it look pristine. Restoration is controversial, since it often involves some irreversible change to the original material of the artwork with the goal of making it "look good." The attitude that has developed in recent years with the development of conservation is to attempt to make all restoration reversible.

The use of watercolor paints to inpaint damages on fresco is an example of a technique utilized to achieve almost complete reversibility. This is the technique used in the 20 year restoration of Da Vinci's "The Last Supper" in Milan. One of the most popular inpainting techniques used today is the Tinted Varnish Treatment. This process is done once the piece is fully cleaned and varnished. This last step in the restoration process is to then go into spots where original paint may be missing, or where patched holes and other irregularities may lay. The restorer then goes in with tinted varnish over the top of the non-tinted varnish. This gives the illusion that the spots have been "re-painted", while in fact it is just a spot of tinted varnish. Most commonly "stippling" is used while using tinted varnish, in order for light to reflect similar to paint. This is done by using tiny dots in a row for variance.

24 **What is the topic of the passage?**

① Controversial art restoration.
② Damaging art restoration.
③ Modern art restoration.
④ Concepts of art restoration.

25 **How has art restoration changed, according to the passage?**

① Previously, art was restored for aesthetic purposes and with no thought to the future.
② Art restoration was originally done by anyway with a paintbrush.
③ Restoring art used to be considered highly insulting to the original artist.
④ Now, art restoration seeks to improve on the original painting.

26 **Choose the correct statement from among the following.**

① The current method of art restoration does not involve repainting pieces, but gives the impression it has been done.
② The original painting is never fully cleaned in order to protect it from further degradation.
③ Restoring artwork is quite a quick process if you know how to do it correctly.
④ Art restoration recently has tended to move towards updating art for the current times.

27–30

According to the benefits principle of tax fairness, those who benefit from public spending should bear the burden of the tax that pays for that spending. For example, those who benefit from a road should pay for that road's upkeep, those who fly on airplanes should pay for air traffic control, and so on. The benefits principle is the basis for some parts of the U.S. tax system. For example, revenue from the federal tax on gasoline is specifically reserved for the maintenance and improvement of federal roads, including the Interstate Highway System. In this way motorists, who benefit from the highway system, also pay for it. The benefits principle is attractive from an economic point of view because it matches well with one of the major justifications for public spending-the theory of public goods. If government's role is to provide people with goods that could not otherwise be made available, it seems natural to charge each person in proportion to the benefits he or she gets from those goods.

Practical considerations, however, make it impossible to base the entire tax system on the benefits principle. It would be too cumbersome to have a specific tax for each of the many distinct programs that the government offers. Also, attempts to base taxes on the benefits principle often conflict with the other major principle of tax fairness: the ability-to-pay principle, according to which those with greater ability to pay a tax should pay more. <u>The ability-to-pay principle is usually interpreted to mean that high-income individuals should pay more in taxes than low-income individuals</u>. Often the ability-to-pay principle is used to argue not just that high-income individuals should pay more taxes but that they should pay a higher percentage of their income in taxes.

27 **What is the passage mainly about?**

① Two points of view that have been proven beneficial to lower-income households.

② Two suggestions for ways in which the government can generate more tax income.

③ Two tried and tested taxation principles that have been discarded.

④ Two major principles that govern tax implementation.

28 **Which of the following is the correct difference between the benefit principle and the ability-to-pay principle?**

① The first one is concerned with economic programs while the second one is more focused on welfare programs.

② One is trying to being more benefits to society while the other is trying to impose strict controls on the benefits.

③ The former focuses on how much a person uses; the latter focuses on how much a person can afford.

④ The benefits principle is generally considered to be fairer than the ability-to-pay principle.

29 **Choose the one that correctly paraphrases the underlined.**

① People who have more money but don't want to pay more than poorer people should teach others to interpret the ability-to-pay principle in a different way.

② The most common interpretation of the ability-to-pay principle is that those who can pay more should pay more.

③ In order to interpret the ability-to-pay principle best it is important to remember that rich and poor people are being asked to pay the same amount.

④ The ability-to-pay principle means that when poor people cannot pay their taxes, rich people should help them.

30 **Why is the benefits principle not used universally, according to the passage?**

① Those in charge of government programs are not able to work together to organize it.

② It is not realistic to organize a separate tax for each government program.

③ Working out the specifics needed to be successful is not required.

④ The people in charge do not think this system is the best possible one.

12 Practice Test

Read the following passages and answer the questions. **[01~30]** (제한 시간: 45분)

01–03

It's a fact of life that age slows mental processing as well as working memory, the everyday recall we take for granted when we make coffee, set down our keys, or go shopping. Often aggravated by impaired sight and hearing, elders respond more slowly to an external stimulus, be it a question, a loud noise, or a funny joke. Older brains take longer to learn new things as well. And recent studies show that for the same task, thinking pathways differ. Functional MRI and other brain imaging, which can map activity during problem solving, indicate that elders use more and often different regions of their brain, <u>giving credence to a common parental lament</u> — the young just think differently.

In an ever faster world, slower thinking can make seniors lose confidence and fear they're destined for Alzheimer's disease. Not necessarily so. Many qualities of natural aging start in the 20s, becoming evident only in the seventh or eighth decade. But blunted reaction times and diminished spatial orientation can make once easy tasks hard — like driving a car. Contrary to what one might think, it's not the teens but the seniors who account for most fatal car accidents. Taking a left turn with oncoming traffic is especially treacherous for them. And there's good reason that ATM machines and security lines at airports flummox older people, especially when a line of impatient whippersnappers gathers behind.

01 Which of the following is correct, according to the passage?

① ATMs are easy for old people to use.
② Young people fear Alzheimer's disease when they start natural ageing.
③ It is hard for an old person to learn a new skill.
④ Natural ageing does not start until your 70s or 80s.

02 What cannot be inferred from the passage?

① Old people do not have the same reaction times as the young.
② Elders don't always get jokes immediately.
③ Elders are more dangerous on the road than young people.
④ Old people do not enjoy the company of young people.

03 Which of the following closely resembles the underlined?

① showing the truth in a common complaint of parents
② making parents look more credible when they talk
③ encouraging parents to try to understand their kids better
④ giving confidence to parents when they scold their children

04-06

Astrology is a group of systems, traditions, and beliefs which hold that the relative positions of celestial bodies and related details can provide useful information about personality, human affairs, and other terrestrial matters. A practitioner of astrology is called an astrologer or an astrologist. Numerous traditions and applications employing astrological concepts have arisen since its earliest recorded beginnings in the 3rd millennium BC. Although contemporary scientists consider astrology a pseudoscience or superstition, astrology has played a role in the shaping of culture, early astronomy, the Vedas, The Bible and various disciplines throughout history. Astrology and astronomy were often indistinguishable before the modern era, with the desire for predictive and divinatory knowledge one of the primary motivating factors for astronomical observation. Astronomy began to diverge from astrology after a period of gradual separation from the Renaissance up until the 18th century. Eventually, astronomy distinguished itself as the scientific study of astronomical objects and phenomena without regard to the astrological understandings of these phenomena.

Astrologers believe that the movements and positions of celestial bodies either directly influence life on Earth or correspond somehow to events experienced on a human scale. Modern astrologers define astrology as a symbolic language, an art form, or a form of divination. Despite differences in definitions, a common assumption of astrology is that celestial placements can aid in the interpretation of past and present events and in the prediction of the future.

04 Which of the following is correct?

① The Bible speaks out strongly against astrology.
② Astronomy and astrology are still very similar today.
③ Astrologers believe that life on Earth affects the movements of celestial bodies.
④ Contemporary scientists have no time for astrology.

05 Why did people start to look at the skies?

① They had seen strange things in the sky.
② People wanted to be able to predict the future.
③ They wanted to be astrologers.
④ They were motivated by others.

06 What can be inferred about astrology?

① Astrology is becoming a widely accepted science.
② Criminals can be caught using astrological predictions.
③ It is possible to understand human behavior through astrology.
④ It was created through a need to explore astronomy further.

07-10

Under the larger discipline of rhetoric (the study of persuasion in all its forms), students in antiquity spent years acquiring a strategic understanding of how to temper logic, emotions and words with poise. Speaking well depended upon learning how to analyse all sides of an argument and assaying all possible avenues of commonality with one's audience before expressing an opinion. Similar to our approach to reading and writing today, speech training was a comprehensive, critical approach to knowledge, with an additional emphasis on psychology and social interaction.

The average American today speaks around 16,000 words a day. If you consider the role of speech in family life, social interactions and on the job, it's easy to see that now, as much as ever, the ability to communicate effectively is the single most critical skill we possess. If we speak in ways that are off-putting, vague or hard to understand, it doesn't matter how smart, hardworking or even good we might be: people will find us difficult to understand and work with. Our usefulness to others will decline with every strained interaction. By contrast, if we speak clearly and well, people will find us easy to understand. They'll 'get' us. They'll like us.

Recently, I worked with an architect who complained: 'I went to school for years, thinking that after graduation, my job would be to design stuff. The reality is that probably 90 per cent of my time goes towards explaining ideas, working on presentations and managing discussions between teams and clients.' Her observation holds true across virtually every advanced occupation. Brilliant as you might be while toiling at your work station, and as important as your solo endeavors are, your social and team value is judged by your ability to skillfully handle phone calls, Zoom meetings, sales and technical presentations, and client interactions. If this sounds far-fetched, how many high-ranking executives can you recall who have poor public speaking skills?

Given the importance of clear, effective speech, ____________________. Yet for most of us, at least in the West, education consists of 12 to 20 years' reading, writing and solving mathematics problems – on paper. As our society has become increasingly knowledge – and information-based, rhetoric and speech instruction have fallen almost entirely out of favour. Many of us graduate unprepared to practise the central activity of our lives, and speech remains the most important subject we've never thought about.

07 **What's the main idea of the passage?**

① As speak ever more in life, our business and personal spheres will be compromised.
② Our speaking skills are in danger of serious degradation if we continue as we are.
③ We are no longer taught to practise something that we spend most of our lives doing.
④ We spend most of our lives speaking and getting to know others around us.

08 **How did the architect mentioned in the passage not foresee her work life?**

① She did not realize how much her designs would rely on the input of others.
② She thought that architects would have a quiet life, but actually they have to be very social.
③ She guessed that she would spend much time designing things but more time explaining.
④ She assumed that she would mainly design things, but she has to communicate more.

09 **According to the passage, which of the following is true?**

① The more we communicate unsatisfactorily, the more we will cultivate ourselves.
② The top people typically in business possess effective communication skills.
③ Poor communication skills can be covered up by intellect.
④ Every occupation needs good speaking skills to succeed.

10 **Which best completes the sentence?**

① you'd think we'd spend lots of time learning to do it in school
② we excel at it before we have even learned other skills
③ children are growing up with a more effective communication ability
④ the value of education is dropping as more focus is put on the wrong things

11-13

When Diane Lewis saw Big's Furniture's sign proclaiming that no interest would be charged until 2015, he was tempted into the year-end liquidation sale in Henderson, Nev. With her sons playing nearby, she said that she couldn't resist coming in as they needed a new bedroom set to replace their old one. With such a deal, they could afford it. Lewis' husband had been out of work for 8 months before recently finding something, and she was suffering as much as anyone else in the area. Although they are two months behind on their mortgage payments and, all told, they owe roughly $20,000 on credit cards, she remains optimistic about getting through it. She knows she should wait a bit, but the offer seems very good and she hopes they will be approved, so she can buy something. 2015 seems so far away, anyway, says the hairdresser. This kind of behavior is nothing new. Hard-hit consumers were claiming frugality was the way forward only just last year, but all has been forgotten. The terrible economic downturn that swept over the nation brought about promises of saving and refraining from indulgences in order to be more like their grandparents ______________________________. However, diets are made to be broken, and so were these promises.

11 What's the topic of the passage?

① A good deal in Nevada
② Breaking the resolution of frugality
③ Getting a new job in the bad economy
④ Credit card debt

12 Choose the true statement.

① Diane Lewis thought this was the perfect time to make a purchase.
② Diane Lewis was able to make all of her payments on the bedroom set.
③ Americans don't believe the lifestyle their grandparents endured in the Great Depression.
④ Last year consumers said that they were going to be more frugal.

13 Which of the following best completes the sentence?

① and stave off the effects of the Great Depression
② although their grandparents had not warned them about how to go about it
③ who suffered the same or worse in the Great Depression
④ which was not to say that they were happy about the prospect

14-16

Kids these days. They don't get married. They don't buy homes. And, much to the dismay of the world's auto makers, they apparently don't feel a deep and abiding urge to own a car. Recently, the New York Times pulled back the curtain on General Motors' recent, slightly bewildered efforts to connect with the Millennials — that giant generational cohort born in the 1980s and 1990s whose growing consumer power is reshaping the way corporate America markets its wares. Unfortunately for car companies, today's teens and twenty-somethings don't seem all that interested in buying a set of wheels. They're not even particularly keen on driving. The Times notes that less than half of potential drivers age 19 or younger had a license in 2008, down from nearly two-thirds in 1998. The fraction of 20-to-24-year-olds with a license has also dropped. And according to CNW research, adults between the ages of 21 and 34 buy just 27 percent of all new vehicles sold in America, a far cry from the peak of 38 percent in 1985. At a major conference last year, Toyota USA President Jim Lentz offered up a fairly doleful summary of the industry's challenge. "We have to face the growing reality that today young people don't seem to be as interested in cars as previous generations," Lentz said. "Many young people care more about buying the latest smart phone or gaming console than getting their driver's license." The billion-dollar question for automakers is whether this shift is truly permanent, the result of a baked-in attitude shift among Millennials that will last well into adulthood, or the product of an economy that's been particularly brutal on the young.

14 **What's the topic of the passage?**

① Buying a car is not as important to young people as it used to be.
② A driver's license is more difficult to attain now than before.
③ Automakers need to reduce their prices.
④ Owning a car is a status symbol for Millenials.

15 **What does the underlined idiom a far cry mean?**

① sadly
② similar to
③ very different
④ consistent with

16 **What can be inferred from the passage?**

① Younger people will eventually buy cars.
② There is no market for young buyers.
③ The auto industry is very concerned.
④ There is nothing to be done to change the attitudes of youth.

17-20

Justice as fairness aims to describe a just arrangement of the major political and social institutions of a liberal society: the political constitution, the legal system, the economy, the family, and so on. The arrangement of these institutions is a society's basic structure. The basic structure is the location of justice because these institutions distribute the main benefits and burdens of social life, for example who will have which basic rights, who will have opportunities to get what kind of work, who will receive social recognition, what the distribution of income and wealth will be, and so on.

The form of a society's basic structure will have profound effects on the lives of citizens, influencing not only their prospects but more deeply their goals, their attitudes, their relationships, and their characters. Institutions that have such pervasive influence on people's lives require justification. Since leaving one's society is not a realistic option for most people, one cannot say that citizens have consented to the arrangement of their institutions by staying in the country. And since the rules of any basic structure will be coercively enforced, often with serious penalties, the demand to justify the imposition of any particular set of rules intensifies further.

In setting out justice as fairness Rawls assumes that the liberal society in question is marked by ____________________ as described above, and also that it is under reasonably favorable conditions: that there are enough resources for it to be possible for everyone's basic needs to be met. Rawls makes the simplifying assumption that the society is self-sufficient and closed, so that citizens enter it only by birth and leave it only at death. He confines his attention mainly to ideal theory, <u>rescinding from questions such as those of criminal justice</u>.

17 **What's the purpose of the passage?**

① To encourage citizens to follow Rawls and leave their society

② To break down the walls of society's structure

③ To petition for change to the basic rights of society's citizens

④ To review Rawls' theory of society

18 **Which of the following is correct, according to the passage?**

① Institutions that have an effect on our lives do not really need to be justified.

② The structure of society affects every part of humans' lives.

③ Most people can leave their society if they do not like it.

④ People who don't like society's rules are applauded.

19 **Which of the following means the same thing as the underlined?**

① trying to answer criminal justice issues

② avoiding questions about criminal justice

③ prescribing solutions for criminal justice problems

④ returning again to criminal justice theories

20 **Which of the following best fits the blank?**

① the distribution of income and wealth

② the closed society

③ any particular set of rule

④ reasonable pluralism

21-23

For example, last spring I received an email telling me that the first prominent review of a new book of mine had appeared: It was in *The Times of London*. Eager to read the review, I clicked on a hyperlink, only to run into a pay wall. Still, I was tempted by an offer to take out a one-month trial subscription for the price of just £1.

As both a consumer and producer of newspaper articles, <u>I have no beef with pay walls</u>. But before signing up, I read the fine print. As expected, I would have to provide credit card information and would be automatically enrolled as a subscriber when the trial period expired. The subscription rate would then be £26 (about $40) a month. That wasn't a concern because I did not intend to become a paying subscriber. I just wanted to read that one article.

But the details turned me off. To cancel, I had to give 15 days' notice, so the one-month trial offer actually was good for just two weeks. What's more, I would have to call London, during British business hours, and not on a toll-free number. That was both annoying and worrying. As an absent-minded American professor, I figured there was a good chance I would end up subscribing for several months, and that reading the article would end up costing me at least £100.

I spoke to Chris Duncan, a spokesman for *The Times of London*. He said his company wanted readers to call before canceling to make sure that they appreciated the scope of the paper's coverage, but when I pointed out the inconvenience this posed to readers outside Britain, he said that the company might rethink that aspect of the policy. In my opinion, the offer was misleading, not transparent; opting out was cumbersome; and the entire package did not seem to be in the best interest of a potential subscriber, as opposed to the publisher.

21 **What does the underlined mean?**

① I have no problem with pay walls.
② I do not care for pay walls.
③ I think pay walls are unjustified.
④ I believe pay walls should be widespread.

22 **What is the purpose of the passage?**

① To put people off becoming subscribers.
② To encourage readers to subscribe to newspapers.
③ To explain why the writer didn't become a subscriber.
④ To dissuade newspapers from asking for subscriptions.

23 **What is implied about Chris Duncan?**

① He knows that the system needs to change but doesn't have the will to change it.
② He is trying his best to change things but his hands are tied by those above him.
③ He will rethink about the repercussions of the policy on international subscribers.
④ He is only concerned about the business of making money and not on journalism.

24-26

Continuing from our conversation around housing segregation and the language employed by those with power I think it's worth thinking some about the text of this petition: "As moral, religious and law-abiding citizens, we feel that we are unprejudiced and undiscriminating in our wish to keep our community a closed community — to protect our own." The petition was put out in 1957, as Levittown sought to stave off integration. What's important to note is that we are well into post-war America and there is some social sanction emerging against prejudice and discrimination. What the petition does is effectively endorse prejudice and discrimination while claiming not to.
Another example: "We favor racial integration, but only at such time the negro shows he is ready for it." Anyone familiar with the popular notion that talking about racism makes one racist will recognize the tactic. It's important to understand that the form is old. As social sanction emerged against slavery after the Civil War, you found former slaveholders insisting that the War actually wasn't about slavery — even as they sought to erect Black Codes which effectively perpetrated slavery.

24 **What's the passage mainly about?**

① The side effects of the Civil War that are still felt throughout America.
② Those who claim to be against racism but actually seek to perpetuate it.
③ Society's acceptance that slavery was not humane.
④ The new prejudices that have replaced the old ones.

25 What was the previous passage about?

① Petitions against racism
② Powerful people's homes
③ Corrupt people in power
④ Racism in housing situations

26 All of the following are true, except ____________________.

① the Civil War was begun as a response to the passing of the Black Codes
② former slaveholders tried to make people believe that the war was not based on slavery and race
③ the petition was meant to fight against integration
④ the Civil War saw the emergence of opinions against slavery

27–30

What ballet is to football players, mathematics is to writers, a discipline so beguiling and foreign, so close to a taboo, that it actually attracts a few intrepid souls by virtue of its impregnability. The few writers who have ventured headlong into high-level mathematics — Lewis Carroll, Thomas Pynchon, David Foster Wallace — have been among our most inventive in both the sentences they construct and the stories they create.

As anyone who has taken a standardized test in the last half-century knows, math and "language arts" run on parallel tracks for much of one's school career. Both begin with an emphasis on rote memorization of the basics: sentence diagrams, multiplication tables. Later, though, both disciplines become more heady : English class discards grammar in favor of the ideas lurking beneath textual surfaces, while math leaves off earthbound algebra, soaring along the ranges of calculus.

<u>By the time you're old enough to drive, you've likely decided which region of the brain you plan to use in your adult life, and which you want nothing to do with beyond the minimum requirements imposed by modern society</u>. Long gone are the days of the catholic scholar who could quote both Pindar and Newton with ease. As the Cambridge mathematician G. H. Hardy noted in 1940's "A Mathematician's Apology," perhaps the most eloquent defense of the subject on its aesthetic merits, "most people are so frightened of the name of mathematics that they are ready, quite unaffectedly, to exaggerate their own mathematical stupidity."

27 **What is the purpose of the first paragraph?**

① To initialize a movement that commemorates writers who have shown mathematical knowledge in their work.

② To explain how opposites remain far away from each other, yet when combined produce something great.

③ To demonstrate how, with a little bit of effort, it is possible to train your brain to follow both avenues of learning.

④ To congratulate those that have seen fit to attempt to bridge the gap between literature and science.

28 **Which of the following paraphrases the underlined sentence?**

① Once you have reached your adult life, your brain has evolved to a state whereby it will not be changed to learn any new things.

② If you want to give back the minimum to a society that has reared you to the age at which you can drive, improve your brain.

③ When you are considered responsible enough to get behind the wheel of a car, you are responsible enough to make your own life choices.

④ As you reach adulthood, your brain has chosen whether it is more comfortable dealing with math or language arts.

29 **Which of the following sums up the words of G. H. Hardy?**

① If mathematics went by any other name, it would lose its ferocious reputation.

② The idea of mathematics is more frightening than actually doing it.

③ Those that are at ease with mathematics embellish its difficulty in order to frighten others.

④ Mathematics can make even its most ardent admirer shake and quiver in fear.

30 **What do the men Lewis Carroll, Thomas Pynchon, David Foster Wallace have in common, according to the passage?**

① Their abilities in both writing and mathematics went undervalued by their peers, and only appreciated later on.

② All wished to follow a different career path from the ones for which they eventually became famous.

③ None of them studied any formal mathematics, despite all appearances to the contrary.

④ They have all been highly successful in marrying mathematics and writing together.

13 Practice Test

Read the following passages and answer the questions. **[01~30]** (제한 시간: 45분)

01–03

Parlez vous Français? *Habla Español*? *Sprechen sie Deutsch*? Have you ever tried to pick up a foreign language? If so, do you recall the mental gymnastics of grasping an alien grammatical structure that twisted your brain into a syntactical pretzel? Now, let's say you only speak English and are stuck in a situation with someone who only understands mandarin Chinese. Words won't get your messages across, so what do you do? Dredge up your best miming skills and use gestures? With that, you may be able to communicate your immediate needs and emotions, but little else.

________________________________ Human language is a far more complex expression than physical communication. Aside from having millions of words at your disposal, you also have tone and pitch for added effect. Think about the differences in how someone would interpret you silently rubbing your stomach to signal hunger compared to you exclaiming, "I'm famished!" Because of these intricacies, people, including renowned linguist Noam Chomsky, have declared that language is a uniquely human trait that separates us from the rest of the animal world.

01 What does the author say Noam Chomsky believes?

① Humans show their personality through their language.

② Humans are distinguished from animals by their use of language to express themselves.

③ The words that people choose to express themselves tell us a lot about their feelings.

④ Animals have been learning language from humans but are still far behind the human world.

02 What's the passage about?

① The difficulties of learning a new language to communicate with someone

② The ability of humans to show exactly how they are feeling through body language.

③ The benefit of getting your point across through language, as opposed to physical communication

④ Languages that give humans the ability to better express themselves.

03 Which of the following best fits for the blank?

① That brings up the difference between language and communication.

② What is the difference?

③ Let me begin by problematising the relation.

④ It is important to distinguish.

04-06

For many drivers, the open road is not nearly as treacherous as parking lots, driveways or intersections, for these places are where the event known as a "fender bender" is most likely to occur. A fender bender is a minor accident that generally causes minor damage to the vehicles involved, but can still become a major issue for the owners of those vehicles. Most automobile insurance agencies provided coverage for damages and injuries caused by a fender bender, but they also have the right to raise a driver's premiums following the report of even a minor accident. For this reason, it is not unusual for drivers to settle the cost of a fender bender between themselves.

A fender bender is so named because the fenders often receive the bulk of the damage in typical accident scenarios. A driver making a sudden stop at an intersection, for example, may cause another driver to crash into his rear bumper or trunk. Another driver may pull out of a driveway without looking for oncoming traffic, creating a hazard for other drivers. The result could be a low-speed collision on the passenger side. A fender bender type of car accident is also likely to occur in large parking lots, as cars jostle for the best spots or inattentive drivers move in the wrong direction.

The good news is that a fender bender rarely causes major injuries or damages, but the bad news is that most insurance companies require that all accidents, large or small, must be reported. Generally, this means a police officer must come to the scene of a reported fender bender and document all that he or she observes about the accident and drivers involved. Photographs of the damage and position of the vehicles may also be taken by either driver to bolster any future legal claims. While an insurance company may ultimately cover the cost of repairs or medical claims, there are occasionally other legal issues which can arise from a fender bender.

04 **Why do people like to avoid their insurance company in a fender bender according to the passage?**

① They do not want to risk having the raise in premiums.
② They are afraid of what the company might decide about who is responsible.
③ They have a dislike of the police.
④ No one has time to wait around for police and insurance people.

05 **Which of the following is incorrect according to the passage?**

① Photos are taken at accidents for legal reasons.
② Police have to be involved if the accident is reported.
③ If a fender bender happens it is very likely to occur in parking lots.
④ Police hate having to deal with such minor accidents so people handle them privately.

06 **Why are these accidents called "fender benders" according to the passage?**

① People end up bending their fenders after the accident.
② People get bent out of shape when they happen.
③ They usually involve just the bumper area of the car.
④ They are almost always occurring in areas where cars can come in contact with each other.

07–10

A growing number of companies known for their hard-nosed approach to business — such as GE, Google, IBM, Intel, Johnson & Johnson, Nestlé, Unilever, and Wal-Mart — have already embarked on important efforts to create shared value by reconceiving the intersection between society and corporate performance. Yet our recognition of the transformative power of shared value is still in its genesis. Realizing it will require leaders and managers to develop new skills and knowledge — such as a far deeper appreciation of societal needs, a greater understanding of the true bases of company productivity, and the ability to collaborate across profit/nonprofit boundaries. And government must learn how to regulate in ways that enable shared value rather than work against it.

Capitalism is an unparalleled vehicle for meeting human needs, improving efficiency, creating jobs, and building wealth. But a narrow conception of capitalism has prevented business from harnessing its full potential to meet society's broader challenges. The opportunities have been there all along but have been overlooked. Businesses acting as businesses, not as charitable donors, are the most powerful force for addressing the pressing issues we face. The moment for a new conception of capitalism is now; society's needs are large and growing, while customers, employees, and a new generation of young people are asking business to step up. The purpose of the corporation must be redefined as creating shared value, not just profit *per se*. This will drive the next wave of innovation and productivity growth in the global economy. It will also reshape capitalism and its relationship to society. Perhaps most important of all, learning how to create shared value is our best chance to legitimize business again.

07 **What's the purpose of the passage?**

① To show people that capitalism has always had and will always have society's best interests at heart.

② To recommend that more people work for businesses that are trying to answer society's problems.

③ To encourage people to take a new look at capitalism and consider a different future for businesses.

④ To disseminate information on a new kind of capitalism that will take over society.

08 **Which of the following is incorrect, according to the passage?**

① The future of capitalism lies in businesses working together for the good of society.

② A wrong perception of capitalism has meant it could not do the good that it was able to.

③ Long-held ideas will need to be rethought if this new kind of capitalism is to succeed.

④ The original concept of capitalism will be fought for and will thrive again.

09 **What can be inferred from the passage?**

① Society needs to reevaluate its knowledge of capitalism and what it can do for us.

② Big businesses face an uphill struggle against government who seek to destroy capitalism.

③ Society needs to learn to look after itself before it allows somebody to do it for them.

④ Society understands how capitalism can work, but those in power need to catch up.

10 **Which of the following best resembles the underlined sentence?**

① When a business merely makes profits, it will no longer one that society wishes to identify itself with.

② A business should be something that has mutual dependence with society, instead of profiting from it.

③ Having defined the purpose of a business, it is up to the business to prove its worth to the society it profit from.

④ Being reliant on society for its success is not a strong position for a business.

11-13

In more than half of the families, students talked about education being a "family matter," causing frequent friction and tension at home. Another area of conflict around education reported by students was that their parents often had very strong emotional reactions to their "failures" in school, including getting angry and yelling. Another common source of conflict was parents' comparisons of their children with others who were academically superior to them, with students recognizing that their parents often used this kind of comparison to motivate them to perform better but admitting it often had the opposite effect.

Even more concerning, says Qin, is that for many children, such constant comparisons can lead to problems with self-esteem and even depression. Take the case of Ming, who reported that his parents' constant comparison and pressure was unbearable and had a very negative influence on his mental health, "it's just like you can't feel like you can function and like yeah, usually after my parents lecture me, I feel like I, like usually, the least that affected me would be like low self-esteem, but the worst would be like, like real depression. Like the kind that you can't function anymore."

11 **What advice for parents can be drawn from the passage?**

① Allow your children to do what they want.

② Give positive reinforcement to children.

③ Always apologize after being angry at your child.

④ Be aware of depression in your child when they are doing poorly in school.

12 Which of the following is true according to the passage?

① Children always do better once motivated by parents, regardless of motivational techniques.

② There are very few ways to get through to children other than yelling.

③ Educational shortcomings are a source of friction between most parents and children.

④ Yelling at children has little effect because children seldom listen to their parents.

13 What is the main idea of the passage?

① Children hate being scolded by their parents.

② Most parents do things the best way they know how.

③ In spite of attempting to help many parents harm their children's education.

④ Education should not be so important that it hurts children.

14–15

While developing programs to help America emerge from the Great Depres- sion, Roosevelt also needed ______________________ and restore the confidence of Americans and to gain their support for the programs of the New Deal, including the NRA. One of the ways FDR chose to accomplish this was through the radio, the most direct means of access to the American people. During the 1930s almost every home had a radio, and families typically spent several hours a day gathered together, listening to their favorite programs. Roosevelt called his radio talks about issues of public concern “Fireside Chats.” Informal and relaxed, the talks made Americans feel as if President Roosevelt was talking directly to them. Roosevelt continued to use fireside chats throughout his presidency to address the fears and concerns of the American people as well as to inform them of the positions and actions taken by the U.S. government.

14 **How did Roosevelt use the radio to strengthen his presidency?**

① He made the people feel that he was talking directly to them, addressing their concerns, and standing together with them.

② He used the radio to broadcast shows that deliberately, and subconsciously, made the listeners more supportive towards his government.

③ He pledged to support the free education of the people by making sure the radio educated them on issues important to them.

④ He spoke on the radio of the things his opposition wanted to smear his name with, and encourages the listeners to stand up against gossip.

15 **Which of the following best fits the blank?**

① to use his propaganda

② to suppress the communist

③ to deal with his people

④ to calm the fears

16–17

A distinguished man should be as particular about his last words as he is about his last breath. He should write them out on a slip of paper and take the judgment of his friends on them. He should never leave such a thing to the last hour of his life, and trust to an intellectual spirit at the last moment to enable him to say something smart with his latest gasp and launch into eternity with grandeur. No--a man is apt to be too much fagged and exhausted, both in body and mind, at such a time, to be reliable; and maybe the very thing he wants to say, he cannot think of to save him; and besides there are his weeping friends bothering around; and worse than all as likely as not he may have to deliver his last gasp before he is expecting to. A man cannot always expect to think of a natty thing to say under such circumstances, and so it is pure egotistic ostentation to put it off. There is hardly a case on record where a man came to his last moment unprepared and said a good thing hardly a case where a man trusted to that last moment and did not make a solemn botch of it and go out of the world feeling absurd.

16 **What does the author say it is to put off preparing your last words?**

① It is a good thing to do as there are many other issues to attend to.
② It is a display of over self estimation to think you are capable of not preparing them.
③ It is the most inappropriate thing a person could do.
④ It is rather inconsiderate of those who will be present to listen to your last words.

17 **What is the best title for the passage?**

① Last words of great men.
② The best thing to do before death.
③ How best to prepare yourself for your last day.
④ The path to a well deserved afterlife.

18-20

After years of telling us to eat our fruits and vegetables, companies are increasingly suggesting that we also put produce on our faces. From apple eye cream to raspberry serum, skin-care products contain whole-food ingredients — along with claims that they reduce puffiness, erase redness or smooth wrinkles.

In theory, adding plant ingredients to creams and moisturizers makes sense, experts say. Fruits and vegetables are full of antioxidant compounds that afford them natural protection from sun, pollution, smoking, insects and other damage — and if they work for plants, why not for us? But be warned: Products need to be formulated carefully to ensure that ingredients remain active and penetrate the skin. Often, a food item that seems promising in a test tube breaks apart when it hits the air or loses its benefits when mixed with other ingredients.

"The big issue is that a food may be great when taken by mouth," says Leslie Baumann, a dermatologist, author and researcher in Miami, "but there are all sorts of reasons why that doesn't mean it's going to be great when you put it on topically."

18 **What's the main idea of the passage?**

① Food products added to skincare seems like a good idea, but it doesn't automatically translate well.

② If food is good for us to take into our bodies, it is good to put on our bodies.

③ How to ensure that products made from produce have the best possible ingredients.

④ Why people would ever believe that food can be used in skincare products.

19 **What do companies claim that skincare products infused with food can do?**

① Even out the skin to reduce the appearance of wrinkles.
② Extend the depth of the red color that appears on the skin.
③ Pinch the skin to give a puffier, younger-looking glow.
④ Demolish the existence of harmful bacteria on the surface.

20 **What is the best subject for the preceding paragraph?**

① The high number of antioxidants found in certain fruits and vegetables
② The importance of getting enough fruits and vegetables in our diet.
③ The beauty secrets that companies know but withhold from us.
④ The harm that our skin takes from modern urban lifestyles.

21–23

Banks make it possible for any individual depositor to withdraw funds whenever he or she wants. Yet the cash in a bank's vault, and its deposits at the Federal Reserve, wouldn't be enough to satisfy all or even most depositors if they all tried to withdraw funds at the same time. <u>Does this mean that there is something fundamentally dishonest about the banking business</u>? Many people have thought so; every once in a while a prominent critic of the banking industry demands regulations that would stop banks from making illiquid loans. But an analogy may help explain what banks do and why it's productive.

Think about car-rental agencies. Because of these agencies, someone who travels, say, from Atlanta to Cincinnati can normally count on having a car when he or she needs one. Yet there are many more potential travelers to Cincinnati than there are cars available to rent; the rent-a-car business depends on the fact that only a fraction of those potential visitors show up in any given week. There's no trickery involved. Travelers believe they can almost always get a car when needed, even though the number of cars actually available is limited — and ____________________. Banks do the same thing. Depositors believe they can almost always get cash when they need it, even though the amount of cash actually available is limited — and ____________________ too.

21 **What is the passage mainly about?**

① The varied depositors that use banks

② The follies of the banking business

③ The funds in the vaults of banks

④ The logic in the way banks operate

22 Choose the one that correctly paraphrases the underlined.

① What does it mean when the business of banking is threatened by corruption?

② How much more can the banking business get before it is brought back down to earth?

③ Is the whole banking industry inherently fraudulent?

④ Are those in the banking industry going to be allowed to get away with such lying?

23 Which phrase fits in both blanks?

① they are right

② it's a travesty

③ it is to be expected

④ their number is not guaranteed

24-26

With humanity's long proud history of standing firm against natural enemies, sometimes in the face of almost certain defeat and extinction, we would be cowardly and stupid to leave the field on the eve of our greatest potential victory.

Understandably, I have been reading the life of Alfred Nobel — a solitary man, the books say, a thoughtful man. He perfected the release of explosive forces, capable of creative good or of destructive evil, but lacking choice, <u>ungoverned by conscience or judgment</u>.

Nobel saw some of the cruel and bloody misuses of his inventions. He may even have foreseen the end result of his probing — access to ultimate violence — to final destruction. Some say that he became cynical, but I do not believe this. I think he strove to invent a control, a safety valve. I think he found it finally only in the human mind and the human spirit. To me, his thinking is clearly indicated in the categories of these awards.

They are offered for increased and continuing knowledge of man and of his world — for understanding and communication, which are the functions of literature. And they are offered for demonstrations of the capacity for peace — the culmination of all the others.

24 What is the meaning of the underlined phrase?

① It has no controlling factor that comes from a moral or ethical source based on the virtues of the society.
② There is no law that restricts what it can or can't be used for.
③ The ethical and moral standards of the society are not followed by this.
④ It has been left to its own devices for an undetermined amount of time.

25 Which of the following is false according to the passage?

① Nobel set up awards for furthering aspects of developing knowledge.

② Nobel was responsible for bring both a great gift and burden to society.

③ Nobel was clearly a disturbed and unhappy individual.

④ Nobel is no longer alive, but his legacy continues to this day.

26 Which of the following is the best title for the passage?

① Nobel arrived with a bang.

② Who Nobel really was.

③ The life and ambition of Nobel

④ Understanding Nobel

27-30

Some students want to get by with as little work as possible. These are usually the worse offenders, for they are most likely to purchase papers from websites that offer papers for sale. They are most likely to copy and paste large blocks of text from online sources and then fail to acknowledge the sources. They are also most likely to "borrow" entire articles and attempt to pass the articles off as original papers. What is the solution when students are lazy? Sadly, unless they decide to take their studies seriously, <u>the only solution is probably a wakeup call</u>, one that will be delivered in no uncertain terms by an instructor who catches them in the act of plagiarism, rewards them with a failing grade, and perhaps even files charges for academic dishonesty. Then, when they find themselves unable to get into another school because of the grievous "stain" on their academic records, these students will finally realize the seriousness of plagiarism.

Regardless of the seriousness of this academic violation, however, students have always resorted to plagiarism, mainly for the reasons stated but also for other less readily identifiable reasons, and students will continue to do so. After all, it can never be prevented entirely, but if students are educated regarding its possible grave repercussions, perhaps at less a few will make a valiant effort to avoid committing plagiarism, and, ultimately, they will be able to influence their peers.

27 **What is the passage mainly about?**

① Why students feel it is sometimes necessary to plagiarize.

② Why teachers are integral to making students understand why plagiarism is bad.

③ Why students plagiarize and how to prevent it.

④ Why peer influence has such a great effect on discouraging plagiarism.

28 What does the underlined mean?

① Finding out why students fundamentally want to plagiarize is at the core of finding a solution.
② Being confronted by the harsh reality of how those who plagiarize are regarded is the only way to stop it.
③ Merely telling students that plagiarism is immoral is usually enough to put them off doing it.
④ Calling students out for plagiarism early on in their academic life is necessary to teach about the wrongs of it.

29 Who does the passage mainly blame for committing plagiarism?

① Teachers who feel stress to help their students achieve higher grades in order to get higher accolades for themselves.
② Students are under extreme pressure to succeed academically and take on more work than they can complete alone.
③ Students who don't want to do the work that is required to complete a project and get a good grade.
④ Students who do not have a good academic record and need to pull out some high grades to improve their chances of further study.

30 What can be inferred from the passage?

① There will always be some students who see fit to plagiarize.
② Plagiarism can be totally eliminated if teachers work on educating students against it.
③ The seriousness of plagiarism will be reduced as less work is original.
④ Plagiarism will become the norm for those trying to enter the top colleges.

14 Practice Test

Read the following passages and answer the questions. **[01~30]** (제한 시간 : 45분)

01-02

Popper's two-volume work published in 1945 traced the roots of totalitarian thought back to Plato in the first volume, and then analyzed the thought of nineteenth German thinkers George Wilhelm Friedrich Hegel and Karl Marx back to Aristotle in the second. Popper writes in favor of what he terms an "Open Society" or liberal democracy, which he argues is the best form of societal organization which can encompass change without the necessity of bloodshed. In opposition to the Open Society, Popper first castigates Plato for casting his sympathies with the rulers against the common citizens, believing that Plato wished to himself be the philosopher-king which he cites as the supreme aspiration for society, rather than democratic government. In both Hegel and Marx, he attacks their philosophical systems of teleological historicism: their arguments that history and the fate of humanity unfolds according to universal laws. Whether in Hegel's philosophy which saw the World Spirit of history embodied in a singular statesman like Napoleon (which had obvious implications for the rise of Hitler, and which Popper traced to modern fascism), or in Marx's philosophy which held that history unfolded through clashes of economic classes (previously unseen except by Marx), Popper found that their all-encompassing explanations intentionally took out the complexity of modern societies with outcomes made by the individual decisions and wills of myriad actors. He believed that history's ends were indeterminate, and that the study of history could not be developed into a predictive science. Popper's ideas were powerful arguments for roles of freedom of choice in human affairs, ideas very much at the center of the fight against Nazi Germany and Imperial Japan in World War II.

01 **Why were Popper's ideas important?**

① They showed people how statesmen took advantage of the ignorant.
② They were instrumental in galvanizing the working classes to stand up for themselves.
③ They clearly explained how leaders ended up dropping in popularity.
④ They helped in the understanding of freedom of choice to fight totalitarianism.

02 **According to the passage, which of the following is correct?**

① Popper thinks that the best form of society is an open society one with no violence.
② Popper sees totalitarianism as only appearing in the twentieth century.
③ Popper agrees with Hegel and Marx that history happens because of universal laws.
④ Popper believes that history can be predicted since there is only one possible outcome.

03-05

Editors need to put things in the paper they can count on, and they like to put things in the paper that make a difference. Narrative is a hard sell that way. That's why I really encourage you to think about it as a paragraph, a line, a small story. Inch your way there. And the other thing you need to know about editors to get them on your side is if you come to an editor with an abstract concept and say "I want to write a narrative piece," what the editor hears is, "Oh my God, investment of time and pain and no sure delivery of product." And this editor has this yawning, gaping hole that is the white space of the newspaper to think about. If you can learn to deliver up small pieces of narrative along the way while you cover the city council and you bring in a weekend piece which is a profile of one of the council members, or a small narrative of how a certain piece of legislation got passed, and you deliver that time and time again and your editor sees you can do that, pretty soon you buy yourself the right to go and say, "Now I'm going to do a narrative. I want to do a story on X." But it has to be specific, it has to be tied to what's going on in your community.

03 **What is the message of the passage?**

① Politics is not as interesting as human interest stories.
② Newspapers are dependent on the quality of their narratives.
③ Editors have too much control over their journalists.
④ Introduce your desire to do narratives to your editor bit by bit.

04 **Why does an editor fear narrative stories?**

① Narrative stories are short in length but long in production.
② Narratives are rarely pieces that encourage readership to increase.
③ Narratives take a lot of time and the end product is not necessarily guaranteed.
④ Narrative stories end up being too personal to the journalist.

05 **Which of the following is true, according to the passage?**

① Editors love to print an interesting narrative but they just can't find any good ones.
② The intentions of the journalist and the editor are sometimes misunderstood on both sides.
③ Journalists find it difficult to write narratives at the same time as they write everyday stories.
④ Each journalist should take their lives in their own hands and demand narratives immediately.

06-09

Would recession cues increase women's desire to buy these products? Four separate experiments, along with real-world data, all say yes. Our findings consistently supported the lipstick effect, as college-age women, when primed with news of economic instability, reported an increased desire to buy attractiveness-enhancing goods, along with a decreased desire to purchase goods that do not enhance one's physical appearance. Our experiments also found that this increased desire for beauty products, clothing and accessories was fully mediated by a heightened preference for mates with resources.

While many journalists who have written about the lipstick effect have theorized that it represents women's therapeutic spending on cheap indulgences, we found that the lipstick effect applies specifically to products that enhance beauty, even when those products are more expensive. Recession cues increased women's desire to buy high-end cosmetics and designer clothing, but not to buy budget-line beauty products, which were rated less effective at improving one's appearance.

Furthermore, we discovered that the lipstick effect and a woman's desire to attract a mate with resources are unrelated to her independent resource access. Women of both higher and lower socioeconomic status expressed an increased desire to buy luxury beauty products when primed with recession cues. This suggests that an uncertain economic climate leads women to heighten mate attraction effort irrespective of their own resource need.

06 What can you infer from the passage?

① In times of financial pressure, women begin to compare themselves unfavorably with other women.

② Lack of money is linked to the kind of physical appearance she wants her mate to have.

③ Women spend more money on luxury products to let people know they are unaffected by the recession.

④ During a recession, women want to look more attractive to attract a mate with more money.

07 **What's the topic of the passage?**

① How to improve your attractiveness during a recession

② The link between a recession and women's spending

③ Why women spend more when their funds are low.

④ The influence of attractiveness on finding a wealthy mate

08 **Choose the false statement from the following.**

① Women focus their spending on beauty and clothing products rather than buying anything.

② Both budget and high-end beauty lines report higher sales during a recession.

③ Economic uncertainty causes women to seek a mate with solid financial status.

④ It doesn't matter what a woman's personal situation is, she will still buy luxury products.

09 **Who is most likely to have written this?**

① A woman that corroborates the research results.

② A rival research institute looking to discredit the results

③ A journalist investigating the research

④ Somebody who took part in the experiments.

10-12

Despite the fact that most Americans believe our country is still The Land of Opportunity, the greatest meritocracy in the world, the United States is actually a terrible place for fortune-seekers. Chris Hayes, author of the new book Twilight of the Elites: America After Meritocracy, notes that when citizens of different countries are polled about their perception of how easy it is to start off poor and work their way up to wealth, "the U.S. is near or at the top in terms of people who say 'yes.' And yet it is also near the bottom in terms of actual <u>social mobility</u>."

In other words, as Hayes argues in his book, America isn't truly a meritocracy. Sure, the Civil Rights movement, feminism, and equal opportunity laws have helped to remove many of the barriers to success — but people at the top tend to stay at the top, from clique to clique, and generation after generation. "Those who climb up the ladder will always find a way to pull it up after them, or to selectively lower it down to allow their friends, allies, and kin to scramble up," Hayes writes.

The powerful are liable to game systems (like school admissions processes) designed to reward merit; they'll also go to great lengths to maintain their bank accounts and their positions (consider, for instance, just about everyone involved in creating the subprime mortgage crisis). And despite the fact that we are all supposedly born with the same legal rights, the elite are rarely punished for their misdeeds, particularly compared to those lower down on the socioeconomic chain. "The idea that we are a meritocracy is a vast oversimplification, a self-serving and self-justifying one," says Hayes. "If you believe that the model is that those who are smartest and hardest working end up with the most power or the most lucrative jobs, then — one conclusion to draw from that is that the people currently occupying those positions must be meritorious, which I think is an insidious myth."

10 **What is the meaning of the term 'social mobility' in the passage?**

① The ability of a society to move its social standards from one extreme to another
② The movement of social perception from one view to the opposing view
③ The ability of one social group to move freely among another
④ The ability of an individual to rise up in their social status within the society

11 **Which of the following is incorrect according to the passage?**

① Hayes disagrees with the idea that America is a meritocracy.
② The US is near the top in people's actual experiences with social mobility.
③ The elite are usually not punished for their misdeeds.
④ People on top tend to remain there while others are only allowed in if they permit it.

12 **Why, according to the passage, is the U.S. not actually a meritocracy?**

① It is not a democratic country.
② There are no rights for the poor.
③ People can't rise socially based on their ability or efforts.
④ People are not treated equally by those in power unless they want to try harder.

13-15

By chance, I had been an undergraduate at the one college in America with an endowed meagre series of poetry readings. Eliot was good, but most performances were insufferable — superb poems spoken as if they were lines from the telephone book. William Carlos Williams read too quickly in a high-pitched voice, but seemed to enjoy himself. Wallace Stevens appeared to loathe his beautiful work, making it flat and half-audible. (Maybe he thought of how the boys in the office would tease him.) Marianne Moore's tuneless drone was as eccentric as her inimitable art. When she spoke between poems, she mumbled in the identical monotone. Since she frequently revised or cut her things, a listener had to concentrate, to distinguish poems from talk. After twenty minutes, she looked distressed, and said, "Thank you." When Dylan Thomas read, I hovered above my auditorium seat as I heard him say Yeats's "Lapis Lazuli." He read his own poems afterward, fabricated for his rich and succulent Welsh organ. I found myself floating again. In four American visits, from 1950 to 1954, when he died in New York, Thomas read his poems many times at many places, from New York's Poetry Center through dozens of western colleges. Frost's eminence among poetry readers disappeared for a time.

13 **What is the passage mainly about?**

① The superiority of Frost as a poet
② The eccentricities of poets
③ The quality of poetry readings
④ The depression that besets the best poets

14 **Which of the following is incorrect, according to the passage?**

① Wallace Stevens spoke as if he didn't like what he was reading.
② Marianne Moore spoke robotically and without feeling.
③ Dylan Thomas spoke so that people hung on his words.
④ All the audience enjoyed what William Carlos Williams was reading.

15 **Which of the following can be inferred from the passage?**

① Poetry was not given much respect at this particular college.
② Thomas did not like traveling to America, so he only made four short trips there.
③ The performance so exhilarated the author that he forgot reality again.
④ Nobody had ever read "Lapis Lazuli" as well as Thomas read it that night.

16-18

This is a gun country. We are saturated with guns. There are as many as 300 million guns in circulation today (the majority owned legally, but many not) and more than 4 million new guns come onto the market each year. To talk about eradicating guns, especially given what the Supreme Court has said about the individual right to gun-ownership, is futile.

There are, however, some gun control laws that could be strengthened. The so-called gun-show loophole (which is not a loophole at all — 40 percent of all guns sold in America legally are sold without benefit of a federal background check) should be closed. Background checks are no panacea — many of our country's recent mass-shooters had no previous criminal records, and had not been previously adjudicated mentally ill — but they would certainly stop some people from buying weapons.

We must find a way to make it more difficult for the non-adjudicated mentally ill to come into possession of weapons. This is crucially important, but very difficult, because it would require the cooperation of the medical community — of psychiatrists, therapists, school counselors and the like — and the privacy issues (among other issues) are enormous. But: It has to be made more difficult for sociopaths, psychopaths and the otherwise violently mentally-ill (who, in total, make up a small portion of the mentally ill population) to buy weapons.

16 **Which of the following is true according to the passage?**

① Most people in the country want guns to be eradicated.

② Gun ownership is a right that no one in the country wants to give up.

③ Gun control is a major issue in the country.

④ The biggest problem in the country are the illegal guns sold to criminals.

17 **Which of the following is a reason why gun control is difficult to improve in the country?**

① There are many people with mental illnesses that are undocumented who shouldn't be able to have guns.

② There are too many guns to collect.

③ The supreme court will never allow guns to be taken away from the citizens of the country.

④ The people who run gun shows will not stop selling guns in their shows no matter what happens.

18 **What is the ultimate goal for the country according to the author?**

① To remove all guns from the country

② To have the supreme court come to a decision on how to prevent gun violence.

③ To find a way to ensure that those who shouldn't have guns don't get them.

④ To stop all gun violence in the country

19-22

Heterosexual women today, in certain milieus, find themselves placed into one of two categories: too young to settle down, and too old to find a man. There is a window of opportunity to get married, but it is <u>ephemeral almost to the point of non-existence</u>. It falls at a different age according to region, or the idiosyncratic biases of one's circle, but hovers around 27. "Too young" refers not to teen marriage, but to any commitment entered into by a grown woman deemed still a child by those around her.

Here's how it works: A young woman hears from friends and family that she needs to focus on her career or education, not some guy. She is warned of certain dangers: unsolicited male attention; unintended pregnancy, as if intended pregnancy were also a thing; and the desire hardwired into all straight men to turn their girlfriends into 1950s housewives. To entertain the possibility of it being difficult to find a husband, to even utter the expression "find a husband," is to regress to another era. And this advice is incredibly appealing, a rejection of the quaint notion that female heterosexuality is the desire not for men, but for a white picket fence.

And then, suddenly, the message shifts. A not-quite-as-young woman will learn that rather than having all the time in the world to start a family, her biological clock is about to strike midnight. That even if she doesn't want children, she is now on the cusp of being too old to find a husband. Hasn't she heard of the man shortage, which only gets worse with age? 40-year-old men can (as will be news to most 40-year-old men) date any 23-year-old they want. And those degrees, that burgeoning career? Maybe feminist dreams shall be realized, or maybe it was just an elaborate mating strategy, tailored for an era when the highest-status men demand women with educational backgrounds similar to their own.

19 What's the idea of the passage?

① Society decides when it is okay for a woman to have fun and when it is time to stop working.
② The notion of what marriage is to a woman has changed as she has grown up and started a career.
③ Women don't want to entertain the thought of getting married until they are ready in their own mind.
④ Women are told they are too young to settle down and then abruptly told that time is running out.

20 Which of the following does not influence a woman's idea about when to get married?

① Her male friends and family members
② The opinions of those whom she surrounds herself with.
③ The beliefs of her relatives
④ Where she comes from.

21 What can you infer from the passage?

① Women are their own worst enemies since the message to get married is conveyed by other women.
② Every 40 year old man knows that if he desires a young girlfriend, he can get one.
③ Feminists don't want to get married and be labeled by society as attached to a man.
④ It is looked down on for a young woman to desire to marry when she is considered young.

22 Which of the following resembles the underlined?

① it is not noticed it until it has gone
② so short that you'd blink and miss it
③ never existed in the first place, not for a minute
④ as transient in nature as a person who doesn't exist

23-26

College has its skeptics, and the skeptics make good points. Does a four-year university make sense for every student? Probably not. Is the modern on-site college education necessarily the ideal means to deliver training after high school? Maybe not. Vocational training and community colleges deserve a place in this discussion. And we happen to be living through a quiet revolution in higher education.

Here are three quick examples. First, beginning this year, students at MITx can take free online courses offered by MIT and receive a credential for a price far less than tuition if they demonstrate mastery in the subject. Second, the University of Southern California is experimenting with online classrooms that connect students across the country in front of a single professor. Third, there's Western Governors University, a non-profit, private online university that's spearheading the movement toward "competency-based degrees" that reward what students can prove they know rather than how many hours or credits they amass.

Some of these experiments will fail, and some will scale. What's important is that they offer higher ed and retraining that is cheap, creative, and convenient. If we can win the marketing war in neighborhoods blighted by NEETs and deliver a post-high school education to some of those 7 million young people who have disengaged with education and work, we will be spending money to save money.

23 What's the main idea of the passage?

① More needs to be done to help those students who are being left behind by the system.
② Online universities are gaining popularity with students in certain fields.
③ Higher education institutions are not happy with the new crop of online colleges.
④ Traditional on-site university education is not the best choice for everyone.

24 Which of the following best paraphrases the underlined sentence?

① Skeptics make an effort to understand all the points of education.
② Skeptics of college education can earn more points than others.
③ Being skeptical about college can bring you extra points.
④ People who are skeptical about college have some valid points to make.

25 How does the passage conclude?

① Spending more money on education will be financially advantageous in the long run.
② More and more young people are becoming disillusioned with higher education.
③ The efforts of the government to improve higher education will ultimately be successful.
④ 7 million young people need to listen to the university marketing strategies and make better choices.

26 Which of the following can be inferred from the passage?

① MITx is becoming more popular than MIT.
② Higher education will soon be much cheaper.
③ Western Governors University will see its applications rise dramatically.
④ The future of higher education will look very different.

27-30

There are cases where you find clear conflicts between computational efficiency and communicative efficiency. Take a simple case, structural ambiguity. If I say, "Visiting relatives can be a nuisance" — that's ambiguous. Relatives that visit, or going to visit relatives. ________________________, the ambiguity is derived by simply allowing the rules to function freely, with no constraints, and that sometimes yields ambiguities. So it's computationally efficient, but it's inefficient for communication, because it leads to unresolvable ambiguity.

Or take what are called garden-path sentences, sentences like "The horse raced past the barn fell". People presented with that don't understand it, because the way it's put, they're led down a garden path. "The horse raced past the barn" sounds like a sentence, and then you ask what's "fell" doing there at the end. On the other hand, if you think about it, it's a perfectly well formed sentence. It means the horse that was raced past the barn, by someone, fell. But the rules of the language when they just function happen to give you a sentence which is unintelligible because of the garden-path phenomena. And there are lots of cases like that. There are things you just can't say, for some reason. So if I say, "The mechanics fixed the cars". And you say, "They wondered if the mechanics fixed the cars." You can ask questions about the cars, "How many cars did they wonder if the mechanics fixed?" More or less okay. Suppose you want to ask a question about the mechanics. "How many mechanics did they wonder if fixed the cars?" Somehow it doesn't work, can't say that. It's a fine thought, but you can't say it. Well, if you look into it in detail, the most efficient computational rules prevent you from saying it. But for expressing thought, for communication, it'd be better if you could say it — so that's a conflict.

27 **What's the main idea of the passage?**

① Knowing the difference between computational and communicative efficiency is tricky for language learners.
② Language needs to put communicative efficiency in precedence over computational efficiency.
③ There is a difference between something making computational and grammatical sense and something being understood in communication.
④ Language rules can be turned upside down if the user knows how to manipulate them while remaining within the rules of linguistics.

28 **What is a garden-path sentence?**

① A sentence that misleads you into thinking it has a primary meaning, while obscuring its secondary meaning.
② A sentence that leads you to automatically believe it doesn't make sense, but read in a different way it has a second correct meaning.
③ A sentence that has a hidden meaning, not evident to most people, but clear to those who know how to use the language well.
④ A sentence that pretends it is perfectly well-formed but, on closer inspection, does not make any sense at all.

29 **Which of the following can be inferred from the passage?**

① Computational conflicts prevent better communication between speakers of different languages.
② The structure of a sentence has little relevance when considering its ambiguity.
③ If a sentence is ambiguous, it is not sufficient for total communication.
④ People are often duped into creating sentences that are computational efficient, but not communicative.

30 **Which of the following best fits in the blank?**

① It is known that to turn out every case is everything
② Every case known as such has been turned out
③ It turns out in every such case that's known
④ Turning out for every case leads into the unknown

15 Practice Test

Read the following passages and answer the questions. [01~30] (제한 시간 : 45분)

01-02

The notion of polysemy itself is trivial: a lexical item is polysemous if it has more than one meaning. Understanding polysemy, however, is far from trivial; in fact, it constitutes one of the major challenges to the discipline. Given that lexical meaning is a constitutive and distinctive aspect of lexical items, a lexical item should strictly not have more than one meaning. Obviously, there are cases in which one would not admit that they represent one item with several meanings but rather different lexical items, which happen to have the same form; these cases are usually set apart from polysemy and considered as instances of homonymy. If we assume that a given case of lexical ambiguity is an instance of polysemy, i.e., several meanings belonging to the same lexical item, that decision has to be grounded on the fact that these are variants connected by recognizable relations, such as, once again, metonymy and metaphor. Cognitive semantics, in particular the work of Lakoff and others, has contributed substantially to understanding polysemy. According to the cognitivist view, the meaning variants of polysemous words are related by basic cognitive processes, such as metonymy, metaphor or narrowing. Often, though not necessarily, there is a basic meaning variant, from which the other meanings are derived in one or more steps. The meaning variants of a polysemous expression thus form a network of concepts interconnected by basic cognitive relations. One influential model proposed by Lakoff is the notion of a "radial category": a network of meaning variants has a central member, from which ______________________, possibly in several steps. The general idea that the meaning variants of polysemous expressions must be related in a principled way, was developed by, among others, Tyler and Evans in an approach they entitle Principled Polysemy.

01 **What is the main idea of the passage?**

① Examples of polysemy in practice
② Multiple derivations of polysemy
③ A semantic view of polysemy
④ Ways of understanding polysemy

02 **Which best completes the sentence?**

① polysemous meanings can be better understood
② the other meanings are shown to be less substantial
③ all others are derived by modifications of different kinds
④ the other meanings should be distinct in meaning

03-05

Another important requirement for the proper functioning of market capitalism is also not often, if ever, covered in lists of factors contributing to economic growth and standards of living: trust in the word of others. Where the rule of law prevails, despite everyone's right to legal redress of a perceived grievance, if there is more than a small fraction of outstanding contracts that require adjudication, court systems would be overwhelmed, as would society's ability to be governed by the rule of law. This implies that in a free society governed by the rights and responsibilities of its citizens, that vast majority of transactions must be voluntary, which, of necessity, presupposes trust in the word of those with whom we do business — in almost all cases, strangers. It is remarkable that a large number of contracts, especially in financial markets, are initially oral, confirmed by a written document only at a later time, even after much price movement. It is remarkable how much trust we have in the pharmacist who fills the prescription ordered by our physician. Or the trust we grant to automakers that their motor vehicles will run as certified. We are not fools. We bank on the self-interest of our counterparties in trade. Just contemplate how little business would get done if that were not the prevailing culture in which we lived. The division of labor so essential to our standard of living would not exist.

03 What's the purpose of the passage?

① To discuss the reasons that will contribute in economic growth and better societies.

② To explain how understanding financial markets can help us to understand society.

③ To convince that trusting others is essential for society to continue to run smoothly.

④ To persuade people that they should think carefully before doing business with strangers.

04 Which of the following is a true statement, according to the passage?

① Trusting the word of others is not usually thought of as a factor in economic growth.

② Law courts can handle many more cases than they currently do.

③ People rarely do business with strangers.

④ Contracts are almost always written first, and cemented orally later.

05 Why is trust important, according to the passage?

① We make more money when we trust others.

② We enjoy life more when we trust those around us.

③ We like to believe that other people care about life.

④ We need to trust others in order to get things done.

06-09

The content of parents' conversations with kids matters. Children who hear talk about counting and numbers at home start school with much more extensive mathematical knowledge, report researchers from the University of Chicago — knowledge that predicts future achievement in the subject. Psychologist Susan Levine, who led the study on number words, has also found that the amount of talk young children hear about the spatial properties of the physical world — how big or small or round or sharp objects are — predicts kids' problem-solving abilities as they prepare to enter kindergarten.

While the conversations parents have with their children change as kids grow older, the effect of these exchanges on academic achievement remains strong. And again, the way mothers and fathers talk to their middle-school students makes a difference. Research by Nancy Hill, a professor at Harvard University's Graduate School of Education, finds that parents play an important role in what Hill calls "academic socialization" — setting expectations and making connections between current behavior and future goals (going to college, getting a good job). ________________________________, Hill reports, has a greater impact on educational accomplishment than volunteering at a child's school or going to PTA meetings, or even taking children to libraries and museums. When it comes to fostering students' success, it seems, it's not so much what parents do as what they say.

06 **What's the main idea of the passage?**

① Parents should focus on the content of the conversations they have with their kids from early childhood into teens.

② Parents should participate in the day-to-day schooling of their children as much as possible.

③ The only important part of the schooling of a child takes place before he/she even goes to kindergarten.

④ Discussing a child's future with them as early as possible will ensure they are successful later in life.

07 **Choose the incorrect statement from the following.**

① As children grow up, parents find it difficult to change what they talk to them about.

② By discussing number at home, children will have a better awareness of math when they go to school.

③ It is possible to guide your child's abilities by choosing specific subjects to discuss in front of them.

④ Parents have a strong influence on their child's achievements by academically and socially.

08 **Which of the following can be inferred from the passage?**

① Talking about a variety of subjects with your young child will ensure their success in social subjects.

② The children of parents who take no part in communication with them are doomed to fail academically.

③ A set schedule of which subjects need to be discussed at which ages should be followed by parents.

④ If you want your child to succeed in art, you should discuss it with them when they are young.

09 **Which of the following best fits the blank?**

① Picking a conversational tone to use

② Choosing to be a friend rather than a parent

③ Engaging in these sorts of conversations

④ Having a strong and tough demeanor

10-13

<u>The longer the youth job crisis persists, the more severe the consequences will be for the global economy</u>, in both developed and developing nations. Instead of nurturing the labor force of the future, the world is creating an underclass of millions of disaffected workers who lack the skills necessary to support growth for decades to come. For advanced economies, where high costs make the development of top-notch talent even more critical, the damage to competitiveness could hamper these countries' ability to contend with emerging rivals like China and India.

In aging societies, especially in Europe and Japan, youth unemployment makes the burden of funding health care and pensions for retirees even heavier, since the number of taxpaying workers is curtailed and the cost of benefits that governments must provide increases. That puts more strain on governments already buried under debt. Youth unemployment's most potentially lethal consequence: unemployed youths are more likely to engage in terrorist activities and crime, studies have shown. "If you have a growing number of people left behind, there is a cost for society," says Anne Sonnet, senior economist at the Organisation for Economic Co-operation and Development, a Paris-based intergovernmental group. "You run the risk of a jobless generation disconnected from society."

10 Which of the following ideas can be found in the passage?

① Society's widening chasm between those with and those without jobs.

② How China and India intend to draw equal with and overtake hitherto dominant economies.

③ The mind-set of the ageing population who are being blamed for the global economic downturn.

④ Governments with debts so high they cannot put a number on it are trying to harness the ageing population.

11 **Which reflects Anne Sonnet's opinion best?**

① It's risky to have a group of young people who are jobless roaming around society.

② Society will be the loser as jobless young people become more detached from the rest of society.

③ As the number of unemployed youth continues to rise, it's up to the ageing population to remedy the situation.

④ Action needs to be taken now if we are to stop the bleeding away from society of unpoliticized young people.

12 **Which of the following closely resembles the underlined?**

① While the global economy's problems continue to deepen, the youth job crisis is dragged along in its wake.

② As severe as the global economical crisis may be, it is worth considering that the youth job crisis is even worse.

③ If youths persist in hampering job improvement efforts, the global economy will reach boiling point.

④ As youth unemployment continues to dog governments, the cost for the global economy will rise.

13 **Which of the following is NOT a consequence of youth unemployment, according to the passage?**

① Many young people will immigrate to countries where they can find work, leaving their own countries with fewer educated minds.

② Developed countries with high youth unemployment lose their ability to compete with emerging markets.

③ There is an increased risk of terrorist activity from disaffected young people.

④ There are fewer taxes coming into the government coffers to pay for welfare for the elderly.

14-17

Learning about poetry (how to read it, write it, and appreciate it) is an integral part of teaching students about all forms of writing. A poem is not just a place to present a student's grammatical knowledge (in fact, it is often the space to subvert it!). Poetry, more than any other form of writing, trains students to take into account the style of language. This close looking and listening is crucial to writing well in any manner. It would be hard to say that any outstanding essay does not involve meticulous word choice or the ability to persuade a reader through sheer aesthetic prowess. Poetry teaches students how to do this.
In the "Importance of Poetry in Children's Learning," Michael Benton argues that poetry is key to children's learning about language because poems read differently than other forms of writing. Even though contemporary poetry rarely adheres to traditional poetic forms, all poetry (contemporary or otherwise) pays close attention to the sound and form of words. When students develop a deep familiarity with the craft of language in a poetry class, they learn how to express their new ideas in sentences and phrases full of their own style.

14 **Which of the following is not true, according to the passage?**

① You cannot always find correct grammatical structures in poetry.
② Poetry can be a useful tool in a child's linguistic development.
③ The way poetry is constructed stymies ability in other forms of writing.
④ Poetry closely focuses on the ways words are constructed and spoken.

15 Which of the following correctly paraphrases the underlined sentence?

① It is understood as true that a great essay has been produced through both careful word choice and through artistic strength which influences the reader.
② An excellent essay, as everyone agrees, must show that the author has chosen his words carefully and be able to convince a reader of an opposite viewpoint.
③ It's easy to say that if an essay has stunned its reader with great syntax and vocabulary, it is difficult to deny its superiority to other forms of writing.
④ It is exceptionally clear to see that choosing your words carefully when writing an essay will make it more influential over its readers.

16 Which of the following describes the opinion of Michael Benton?

① It is dangerous for children to read poetry as it introduces bad grammar to them at an early age.
② Contemporary poetry bears little to no resemblance with traditional poetry and should be avoided.
③ Children need to learn how to read and appreciate poetry in order to form their own language.
④ Poetry should be taught to all children, but only after they have learned to form their own language.

17 Which of the following ideas could be best discussed next?

① Ways to incorporate the learning of poetry into children's classrooms
② Why children prefer reading poetry to reading other things
③ Whether contemporary or traditional poetry is best for children's learning.
④ How poetry is superior to other forms of writing.

18-20

Organizations trying to decide whether and when to allow people to work remotely are stuck in the last century. In the 1950s, requiring employees to work in the same location made a lot of sense. But we've evolved, as civilizations tend to. Today we have numerous tools that allow us to work from literally anywhere on the planet. We are moving forward, and society is aligned in favor of a 24/7 economy that rewards personal responsibility and freedom. It's not about who's in the office vs. who's gotten a special pass to work outside the building.
Responsibility and freedom. Responsibility for the work, and the freedom to do it in a way that makes common sense. <u>Managers are playing hall monitor instead of getting crystal clear with each employee about delivering measurable results</u>. Managed flexibility is seriously outdated — just paternalistic behavior of granting permission for people to work outside of the 1952 constraints of time and place. Organizations can trust their employees to own their work and manage their time without vintage H.R. policies about office hours or remote working. Managing someone's time is a way of saying, "I don't know how to effectively manage the work, so now I'm going to try to manage you."
Treat people like the adults that they are, and they will act like adults. Treat them like children, and you'll find yourself with a workplace full of people who are watching the clock tick waiting for the bell so they can make a mass exodus. Our advice: Focus on managing the work, not the people. People can manage themselves. Get clear on what needs to get done and how it's being measured, and stop managing how and where people do it. If they don't deliver, they're out. No results? No job.

18 **Which of the following can be inferred from the passage?**

① The new business landscape favors those companies who do not need to worry about their employees.

② Companies that allow their employees total freedom enjoy better business and higher revenues.

③ The modern way of managing should involve both innovations and traditional practices.

④ Showing an employee that you trust them will encourage them to act sensibly and not betray that trust.

19 **What's the opinion of the passage?**

① Managers need to give their employees the freedom they require to get the best results.

② Managers wouldn't have jobs without the employees, so they should treat them better.

③ The focus of managers has been diverted from what it should always have been to employees.

④ Managers need to be monitored sometimes just as much as employees do.

20 **What is the best paraphrase of the underlined sentence?**

① Depending on how a manager speaks to an employee, variable results will be seen.

② If managers did less playing with their employees and got down to some hard work, they would see better end results.

③ It's obvious that managers care more about knowing details of their employees personal lives than they do about getting their work done.

④ Managers need to emphasize the results they want to see from their employees rather than treating them like children and monitoring their time.

21-24

In 2007, the Pew Research Center set out to test whether the wide array of news sources available at that time made people any better informed. The answer : 'Not so much'. Roughly as many people could name the vice president, or their state's governor, as were able to do so in 1989. On some questions, people did better; on others, they did worse. But the bottom line was that people were about as likely to name key leaders, and were about as aware of major news events, as they had been nearly two decades earlier.

Information technology today — constant news on Twitter and Facebook, streaming video on iPhones — makes 2007 seem like the Dark Ages. But Pew Research's "news IQ" quizzes have found that the public continues to struggle with many basic facts about politics and current events. In our most recent quiz, in July, just 34 percent of Americans were able to identify John Roberts as the chief justice of the Supreme Court, from a list that included Harry Reid and the late William Rehnquist. As was the case in the predigital era, college graduates are better informed than those with less education. Yet the swelling ranks of college graduates have not led to a better informed public. Moreover, while education is correlated with increased knowledge about prominent people and news events, it may not confer as much of an advantage as it did in the 1980s.

For people who actively seek out information on politics and current events, the current media landscape provides previously unimagined opportunities for obtaining news and information. Want to watch the presidential debate on your cellphone? Easy. Tweet about it as it is happening? No problem. But the rise of digital news sources is having less of an impact on the millions of Americans who are not that interested in the news, who lack the background to make sense of it, or who simply can't afford the technology.

21 What's the topic of the passage?

① The levels of knowledge that are exhibited in various demographics.
② The effect of current advanced news media on public knowledge.
③ The case for creating even more media outlets to inform a wider public.
④ The consequences on media of people knowing more information.

22 Which of the following is incorrect, according to the passage?

① People with little education still do not know as much as those with higher education.
② The people who used not to be interested in news are not encouraged to find out more now.
③ College graduates know more information now than they did before the digital era.
④ No more people can name the governor of their state now than could before.

23 Which is NOT mentioned as a reason why some are unaffected by increased digital news sources?

① Some people prefer to get their news in ways other than digitally.
② Some people don't have the means to buy products on which to receive news digitally.
③ Some people are not intelligent enough to understand the news.
④ Some people simply don't care about what is happening in the news.

24 Which of the following best paraphrases the underlined sentence?

① As more people wish to go to college, the public is becoming less enamored with graduates.
② A higher number of college graduates than normal means that the public is becoming smarter.
③ Although there are more college graduates these days, it does not mean that the public knows more.
④ If the public wishes to educate itself more, it should go to college in greater numbers.

25-28

The area around the departure gate is crowded, so it's obvious the plane will be full. In fact, it turns out that it's more than full. The gate agent announces that the flight is overbooked and asks for volunteers to give up their seats in return for rebooking on a later flight plus additional incentives, such as $200 toward a future ticket. If not enough volunteers come forward immediately, the incentives are increased. This scene is familiar to any frequent flier. But it didn't always work that way. In fact, it took a couple of economists to teach the airlines how to deal efficiently with overbooking.

On busy flights, airlines have always sold tickets for more seats than actually exist. There's a good reason for this: some people with reservations always fail to show up, and an empty seat is a seat wasted. But sometimes fewer people than expected are no-shows, and a flight ends up overbooked. What happens then? Until 1978, airlines simply "bumped" some of their passengers-informed them that their reservations had been canceled. There were no uniform rules about who got bumped; some airlines, for example, bumped older passengers because they were less likely to complain. Needless to say, those who got bumped were not happy. In 1968, however, the economist Julian Simon proposed a market approach, in which airlines would treat a flight reservation as if a seat were a property right given to the passenger, so that the airlines would have to buy that right back if the plane was overbooked. Airlines didn't think this idea was practical. But in 1978 another economist, Alfred Kahn, was appointed to head the Civil Aeronautics Board, which regulated airlines at that time. He required airlines to use an auction system to deal with overbooking, resulting in the familiar process of asking for volunteers. What's the advantage of this voluntary, market solution? Under the old system, someone who urgently needed to get on the scheduled flight was as likely to get bumped as someone who could easily take a later connection. Since 1978, those who absolutely have to make the flight don't volunteer; those who aren't that anxious to board get something that's worth more to them. The airline pays a cost to get passengers to give up their reserved seats but more than makes up for it in higher overall customer satisfaction. In short, everyone gains. By using property rights to create a market, Simon and Kahn moved that piece of the economy toward efficiency.

25 **What is the main idea of the passage?**

① A solution that was more advantageous to all parties involved.
② Finding a way for the customers to pay less money for better service.
③ Devising regulations that will control what the airlines do.
④ A method of protecting valued customers and neglecting random ones.

26 **Which of the following is true, according to the passage?**

① When passengers do not want to change to a later flight, they are forced to give up their seat.
② There are usually no passengers who voluntarily agree to take a later flight regardless of the compensation.
③ Older passengers often got the short end of the stick when flight bumping was necessary as a result of their age.
④ Selling more tickets than seats available is a fairly new phenomenon that airlines have begun to raise their profits.

27 **How did Alfred Kahn benefit airline passengers?**

① He convinced the airlines to ask people to volunteer rather than previous random method.
② He showed the airlines that passengers would never be completely loyal to one airline.
③ He encouraged airlines to treat some passengers better than others, thereby creating competition.
④ He rose in the ranks of the airline and quickly took on more responsibility.

28 **Which of the following cannot be inferred?**

① Those people who fly a lot these days have seen the overbooking and the bumping auction happen often.
② Julian Simon was a passenger who had been unwillingly bumped and wanted to do something about it.
③ Some passengers do not have tight schedules and are perfectly willing to be bumped to a later flight.
④ People who purchase tickets but do not take the flight prevent others from taking that flight.

29-30

Writers, like everyone else, will welcome an ordered society of peace and plenty; and literature can collaborate with the State that achieves these ends. The state, in its turn, must admit ______________________ of this collaboration — that the writer, however he may serve the State, is still the tribune of the person, the critic of institutions, the agent of change. This must always be his work, and today he has part to play which is even more important and more difficult. His value will be in attempting to redefine the ends for which men desire to live, to salvage from the past what is permanent and set it in its place of honour, to set what is critical, strange, reflective and apparently useless in opposition to what is stereo-typed, practical, obvious and efficient.

29 **What cannot be inferred from the passage?**

① Writers are a unique member of the society.
② The writer is bound to the state and its people in whole.
③ The writer is the recorder of things as they should be.
④ The writer is not a confrontational person.

30 **Choose the one that best fills in the blank.**

① the complementary evidence
② the paradoxical nature
③ the compelling evidence
④ the contradictory nature

16 Practice Test

Read the following passages and answer the questions. [01~30] (제한 시간: 45분)

01

Making a sandcastle is a favorite project of beach-goers of all ages. Begin by digging up a large amount of sand (enough to fill at least six pails) and arranging it in a pile. Then, scoop the sand into your pail, patting it down and leveling it off at the rim as you do. You can now construct the towers of your castle by placing one pail full of sand after another face down on the area of the beach that you have staked out for yourself. Make four towers, placing each mound twelve inches apart in a square. This done, you are ready to build the walls that connect the towers. Scoop up the sand along the perimeter of the fortress and arrange a wall six inches high and twelve inches long between each pair of towers in the square. By scooping up the sand in this fashion, you will not only create the walls of the castle, but you will also be digging out the moat that surrounds it. Now, with a steady hand, cut a one-inch square block out of every other inch along the circumference of each tower. Your spatula will come in handy here. Of course, before doing this, you should use the spatula to smooth off the tops and sides of the walls and towers.

01 **What is the purpose of the passage?**

① To teach someone how to build a sand castle.

② To prove making a castle is easy in the sand.

③ To explain how to pass the time at a beach.

④ To show how useful a pail and scoop can be on a beach.

02-04

To understand what *Blue Ocean Strategy* is, imagine a market universe composed of two sorts of oceans: red oceans and blue oceans. Red oceans represent all the industries in existence today. This is the known market space. Blue oceans denote all the industries not in existence today. This is the unknown market space. In the red oceans, industry boundaries are defined and accepted, and the competitive rules of the game are known. Here, companies try to outperform their rivals to grab a greater share of existing demand. As the market space gets crowded, prospects for profits and growth are reduced. Products become commodities, and cutthroat competition turns the red ocean bloody. Blue oceans, in contrast, are defined by untapped market space, demand creation, and the opportunity for highly profitable growth. Although some blue oceans are created well beyond existing industry boundaries, most are created from within red oceans by expanding existing industry boundaries. In blue oceans, competition is irrelevant because the rules of the game are waiting to be set. It will always be important to swim successfully in the red ocean by outcompeting rivals. Red oceans will always matter and will always be a fact of business life.

02 What is the passage about?

① The effect of modern business strategies on the oceans
② The symbolism of red and blue oceans in the business world
③ The way that rival companies compete to gain the upper hand
④ The unfortunate business life of those who try to win in the business world

03 What is the meaning of the underlined sentence?

① Those who want to succeed in the business world do not care about what happens to their rivals.
② Competition is at the heart of business, but hopefully this is changing.
③ Business life will always include competition and success coming by outperforming one's rivals.
④ A lifetime in business will turn you into somebody who constantly wants to succeed.

04 What's the difference between red and blue oceans, according to the passage?

① Red oceans are concerned with only one type of business; blue oceans are concerned with all the rest.
② Blue oceans nurture imagination and invention; red oceans suppress such ideals.
③ Blue oceans give opportunities to those who have been denied such things; red oceans deny them.
④ Red oceans concern the existing business world; blue oceans concern that which does not exist.

05-08

Daddy's girl is a phrase that can be interpreted in two ways. First, a daddy's girl can be the result of the way in which a man dotes on his daughter, coddling and protecting her and giving her whatever she wants. A daddy's girl knows that she is her father's life and often takes advantage of the fact that he can't stand to see her cry. A daddy's girl can never do anything wrong and is <u>as innocent as the day is long</u>. Because a daddy's girl is the light of her father's life, she may be under lock and key. In fact a daddy's girl may proudly — or not — declare that she is owned by her father. A father might try to shelter his daughter from all the unsavory aspects of life, preventing her from developing her independence.

With the view that she is delicate and helpless, a daddy's girl can easily turn into a little princess. However, the opposite is often true as well. A daddy's girl can learn from her father how to play sports, climb trees, fix things, and so on. In this way, a daddy's girl can also become a tomboy. Many daddy's girls feel frustrated when they reach adolescence and develop an interest in dating, because their fathers rarely think that any boy will ever be good enough to date their daughter.

The second meaning of a daddy's girl is a girl that shows a great particularity for her father and does everything to please him. A daddy's girl puts her father on top of the world where no other man could ever measure up. This type of daddy's girl strives to impress her father, seeking approval, and is highly concerned about how he thinks of her. This situation is a great example of the Electra complex, a psychoanalytic concept that refers to a female's unconscious tendency to form a close attachment to her father and to subsequently exhibit hostility to her mother. The daddy's girl of the Electra complex is comparable to the mamma's boy illustrated in the psychoanalytic concept of the Oedipus complex.

05 What's the best title for the passage?

① Are you a 'daddy's girl'?

② Electra and Oedipus

③ The two sides of the 'daddy's girl' coin

④ The stress of being a 'daddy's girl'

06 Which of the following is false, according to the passage?

① A daddy's girl can be taught to act like a boy by her dad.

② A daddy's girl has negative emotions towards her father.

③ Some daddy's girls spend their lives trying to impress their fathers.

④ Fathers of daddy's girl sometimes make life difficult for them when they start dating.

07 What does the phrase 'as innocent as the day is long' mean?

① innocent for a day at a time

② innocent only when she wants to be

③ innocent all the time

④ innocent in short bursts

08 Which of the following cannot be inferred from the passage?

① Daddy's girls could develop a negative attitude to their mothers.

② Fathers of daddy's girls could have a hard time trusting boyfriends.

③ A daddy's girl would rarely be scolded by her father.

④ Daddy's girls want to find a husband who resembles their father.

09-11

It goes on underscoring the old truth that one man's utopia is another's dystopia — for there is too much variety in human nature for it all to fit one mold. "What has always made the state a hell on earth," says the poet Friedrich Holderlin, "has been precisely that man has tried to make it his heaven."

The notion that we could ever construct a scientific "utopia theory" is, then, doomed to absurdity. Certainly, a "physics of society" can provide nothing of the sort. One does not build an ideal world from scientifically based traffic planning, market analysis, criminology, network design, game theory, and the gamut of other ideas. Concepts and models drawn from physics are almost certainly going to find their way into other areas of social science, but they are not going to make traditional sociology, economics, or political science redundant. The skill lies in deciding where a mechanistic, quantitative model is appropriate for describing human behavior. This is a skill that is still being acquired, and it is likely that there will be embarrassments along the way.

But properly and judiciously applied, physical science can furnish some valuable tools in areas such as social, economic, and civic planning, and in international negotiation and legislation. It may help us to avoid bad decisions; if we are lucky, it will give us some foresight. If there are emergent laws of traffic, of pedestrian motions, of network topologies, of urban growth, we need to know them in order to plan effectively. Once we acknowledge the universality displayed in the physical world, it should come as no surprise that the world of human social affairs is not necessarily a tabula rasa, open to all options.

09 **What is the best topic for the preceding paragraph?**

① The similarities of humans.
② A physics of society.
③ The poems of Friedrich Holderlin.
④ The differences and variety in humans.

10 **Why is one man's utopia another man's dystopia?**

① It is human nature to fight with other humans.
② Humans can be easily categorized and usually fit into one mold.
③ Humans want to be like each other and copy the behavior they see.
④ Human beings vary so much that it is impossible for everyone to like the same things.

11 **According to the passage, which of the following is false?**

① Physical science may help us to avoid making bad decisions in the future.
② Human behavior follows a very simple model, which hardly ever varies.
③ Physics cannot replace over subjects such as sociology, economics or political science.
④ Physical science needs to be applied properly to produce any useful results.

12-14

Wit is a lean creature with sharp inquiring nose, whereas humor has a kindly eye and comfortable girth. Wit, if it be necessary, uses malice to score a point – like a cat it is quick to jump – but humor keeps the peace in an easy chair. Wit has a better voice in a solo, but humor comes into the chorus best. Wit is as sharp as a stroke of lightning, whereas humor is diffuse like sunlight. Wit keeps the season's fashions and is precise in the phrases and judgments of the day, but humor is concerned with homely eternal things. Wit wears silk, but humor in homespun endures the wind. Wit sets a snare, whereas humor goes off whistling without a victim in its mind. Wit is sharper company at table, but humor serves better in mischance and in the rain. When it tumbles, wit is sour, but humor goes uncomplaining without its dinner. Humor laughs at another's jest and holds its sides, while wit sits wrapped in study for a lively answer. But it is a workaday world in which we live, where we get mud upon our boots and come weary to the twilight--it is a world that grieves and suffers from many wounds in these years of war: and therefore as I think of my acquaintance, it is those who are humorous in its best and truest meaning rather than those who are witty who give the more profitable companionship.

12 Which of the following is incorrect?

① Humor is much less acceptable than wit in any situation.
② Wit is a much crueler thing than humor could ever be.
③ Humor is rather comforting in comparison to wit.
④ Wit probably leaves most people feeling stung after it has been employed upon them.

13 What is the best title for the passage?

① Not as subtle as humor, but just as funny.
② The desire for humor over wit.
③ On the difference between wit and humor
④ The weariness of wit in a world of humor

14 What is the difference between wit and humor according to the passage?

① Humor is a much more base and undesired form of exchange among people than wit.
② Wit gives fewer wounds than humor does at the dinner table.
③ Wit requires a much quicker and adept mind than humor, which is a more friendly form of jest.
④ Wit and humor are one in the same; they are just different sides of the same coin.

15-18

But here's where the real debate over America's moral position comes into focus. As the *New York Times* notes, out-of-wedlock births are increasing in much of the developed world — for example, over half of babies in Iceland and Sweden are born to unwed mothers. But according to Wendy Manning, a professor of sociology at Bowling Green State University, "In Sweden, you see very little variation in the outcome of children based on marital status. Everybody does fairly well…. In the US, there's much more disparity."

So out-of-wedlock birth need not correspond to worse outcomes for children. And if it didn't in America, should we still consider out-of-wedlock births a moral problem? One could ask a similar question about religion. While rates of religious participation may be declining in America, young people today have similar moral beliefs as their parents and grandparents. So is the decline in religious observance a moral problem?

When it comes to <u>out-of-wedlock</u> births, the issue is complicated because discouraging these types of the births may be a more efficient way of securing children than the type of nanny-state intervention that can be found in a country like Sweden. But in general, I think the debate over America's moral position comes down to this: Republicans want the best outcomes based on solutions that fit into preconceived notions of what society should look like. So even if there are few tangible harms that point to our moral decay, any move away from their vision of society is evidence of declining virtue. Democrats, on the other hand, are more concerned with outcomes, even if that means upending the way things were (or accepting that they have been upended and cannot be restored).

So in the case of out-of-wedlock births, Republicans would probably see the increase as a moral problem regardless of the outcome. Whereas Democrats might feel more comfortable with, say, promoting a corresponding increase in stable familial relationships outside of marriage. It is a dynamic we've seen elsewhere recently, in regard to issues like gay marriage and contraception. And it leads to a debate over what "moral" really means. If "immoral" means "causing avoidable harm to other people" then gay marriage, pornography, sex, reality TV, soft-drug use and euthanasia are hardly immoral, even if distasteful to some.

15 **What can be inferred from the passage?**

① The U.S. doesn't offer the same amount of support as some other countries.
② The best way to deal with out-of-wedlock births is to try and prevent them.
③ Giving adequate support for these children is not the job of government.
④ There is little to be done in the U.S. that hasn't already been done.

16 **Which of the following best sums up the view points of Republicans and Democrats?**

① One group accepts the change in the family dynamic while the other resists it.
② They are in disagreement on how to help, but both support this new trend.
③ There is little division between the two parties.
④ They both prefer the traditional family unit but Republicans are more accepting.

17 **What is the meaning of the underlined phrase?**

① without your wedding partner
② after being married
③ before marriage
④ not during marriage

18 **Which of the following is incorrect according to the passage?**

① Many countries have children born out-of-wedlock.
② The U.S. has higher rates of out-of-wedlock marriage than any other country.
③ The two political parties in America disagree about out-of-wedlock births.
④ There is a decline in the number of people who go to church.

19-21

Community colleges are typically assumed to be nonselective, open-access institutions. Yet access to college-level courses at such institutions is far from guaranteed: the vast majority of two-year institutions administer <u>high-stakes exams</u> to entering students that determine their placement into either college-level or remedial education. Despite the stakes involved, there has been relatively little research investigating whether such exams are valid for their intended purpose, or whether other measures of preparedness might be equally or even more effective. This paper contributes to the literature by analyzing the predictive validity of one of the most commonly used assessments, using data on over 42,000 first-time entrants to a large, urban community college system. Using both traditional correlation coefficients as well as more useful decision-theoretic measures of placement accuracy and error rates, I find that placement exams are more predictive of success in math than in English, and more predictive of who is likely to do well in college-level coursework than of who is likely to fail. Utilizing multiple measures to make placement decisions could reduce severe misplacements by about 15 percent without changing the remediation rate, or could reduce the remediation rate by 8 to 12 percentage points while maintaining or increasing success rates in college-level courses. Implications and limitations are discussed.

19 What can be inferred from the passage?

① Colleges will continue to follow the same admission rules.
② There will be changes in how college education is structured.
③ The requirements for some colleges may change to allow students based on different criteria.
④ There will be a complete overhaul of the education admissions system to allow all students to enter college.

20 Which of the following are untrue according to the passage?

① There are currently multiple measures taken to ensure students can enter college.
② The current system prevents some students from entering college.
③ Some things can be done to improve student's chances of being accepted into college.
④ Some colleges offer programs for those who could not enter into university.

21 What is meant by the underlined phrase, based on the passage?

① A test that has a great reward.
② A test that not all students can pass.
③ A test that will determine what they can study.
④ A test that has great risk and reward for the student.

22-24

Amazon's culture has been deeply influenced by Mr Bezos's own experiences. A computer-science graduate from Princeton, he returned to his alma mater last year to give a speech to students that provided some fascinating insights into his psychology as an entrepreneur. He explained that he had been a "garage inventor" from a young age. His creations included a solar cooker made out of an umbrella and tin foil, which did not work very well, and an automatic gate-closer made out of cement-filled tyres.

That passion for invention has not deserted Mr Bezos, who last year filed a patent for a system of tiny airbags that can be incorporated into smartphones, to prevent them from being damaged if dropped. Even so, in the 1990s he hesitated to leave a good job in the world of finance to set up Amazon after a colleague he respected advised him against it. But Mr Bezos applied what he calls a "regret minimisation framework", imagining whether, as an 80-year-old looking back, he would regret the decision not to strike out on his own. He concluded that he would, and with encouragement from his wife he took the plunge as an entrepreneur. They moved from New York to Seattle and he founded the company, in time-honoured fashion for American technology start-ups, in his garage.

This may explain why Mr Bezos is so keen to ensure that Amazon preserves its own appetite for risk-taking. As companies grow, there is a danger that novel ideas get snuffed out by managers' desire to conform and play it safe. "You get social cohesion at the expense of truth," he says. He believes that the best way to guard against this is for leaders to encourage their staff to work on big new ideas. "It's like exercising muscles," he adds. "Either you use them or you lose them."

22 **What is the main topic of the passage?**

① The way Mr.Bezos likes to do business
② The influence of Mr.Bezos's life on his business
③ The future of Amazon in the near future
④ The future projects of the founder of Amazon

23 **What is the meaning of the underlined phrase?**

① When you don't do something you forget how to do it.
② The only way to stay in shape is to keep working.
③ The only way to do business is to always work.
④ There is nothing that can be remembered regardless of your practice.

24 **Which of the following is not true according to the passage?**

① Mr.Bezos started his business from his garage.
② There are lots of ways he could have accomplished his goals.
③ There were risks involved when starting a new company.
④ Some people supported his idea while others didn't.

25–28

Adenauer's crowning mercy was that, as President of the Parliamentary Council, he was able to write his own constitution. He took a lot of time and trouble over it and eventually produced one of the best constitutions ever drawn up for a modern state, which skillfully balances sufficient authority for the Chancellor against the entrenched powers of its federal constituents. By comparison with the Weimar constitution it was a masterpiece. For the first elections, set for 14 August 1949, he formed an alliance with Professor Ludwig Erhard, head of the Bizonal Economic Council, whose free market economic philosophy, based on low tariffs, free trade, cheap imports and high exports, was exactly suited to his own political philosophy and was, indeed, already producing results by the summer of 1949.

The British, wrong to the end, assumed the Social Democrats would win easily. In fact the CDU vote was 7,360,000, against fewer than 7 million for the Socialists, and Adenauer, in rejecting the idea of a non-party coalition government, was able to argue that a total of 13 million Germans had voted for free enterprise — that is, for Erhard's ideas — and only 8 million for nationalization. What emerged, after the election, was that Adenauer was in total control of his party (and of Erhard). In getting himself made Chancellor and forming his government he behaved in an authoritative, not to say high-handed, manner. He said that, on doctor's advice, he could only remain in office for two years. He remained for fourteen. The August election was thus one of the critical events of the post-war world. An SPD government, with the economic philosophy and programme it then possessed, could never conceivably have achieved the German Wirtschaftswunder. The Adenauer-Erhard combination was essential to it.

25 **What is the passage mainly about?**

① The problems that would have faced any post-war German government, trying to rebuild the country.

② The victory of Adenauer and his ideals over the Social Democrats in post-war Germany.

③ The CDU proposition to the SPD that resulted in the future post-war German government.

④ The intricacies in the political alliance between Adenauer and Erhard.

26 **Which of the following was not part of the Adenauer-Erhard free market economic philosophy?**

① Imposing low taxes on trading companies

② Bringing goods into the country at a low price, and selling goods out at a high price

③ Allowing consumers to have a say in the variety of imported goods

④ Removing government interference from trading

27 **What can be inferred from the passage?**

① Erhard knew what Adenauer was planning, and tried to stop his grand designs.

② Adenauer and Erhard worked well together, despite their personal dislike of one another.

③ The British had strongly tried to influence the future of Germany's political scene.

④ The Weimar constitution was not considered a well-written, well thought through constitution.

28 **Which of the following best resembles the underlined?**

① His blood, sweat and tears resulted in a constitution that was better than any other modern state enjoyed.

② Modern states were not used to such constitutions being tirelessly thrust upon them.

③ Drawing up a constitution in modern times needed lots of energy and effort channeled into it.

④ The troubles that were taken to make up a modern constitution went to waste as the one that was drawn up was inadequate.

29–30

In simplest terms, what the equation ($E = mc^2$) says is that mass and energy have an equivalence. They are two forms of the same thing: energy is liberated matter; matter is energy waiting to happen. Since c^2 (the speed of light times itself) is a truly enormous number, what the equation is saying is that there is a huge amount — a really huge amount — of energy bound up in every material thing.
You may not feel outstandingly robust, but if you are an average-sized adult you will contain within your modest frame no less than 7×10^{18} joules of potential energy — enough to explode with the force of thirty very large hydrogen bombs, assuming you ________________ and really wished to make a point. Everything has this kind of energy trapped within it. We're just not very good at getting it out. Even a uranium bomb — the most energetic thing we have produced yet — releases less than 1 percent of the energy it could release if only we were more cunning. Among much else, Einstein's theory explained how radiation worked; how a lump of uranium could throw out constant streams of high-level energy without melting away like an ice cube. (It could do it by converting mass to energy extremely efficiently.) It explained how stars could burn for billions of years without racing through their fuel. (Ditto.)

29 **Which of the following fits the blank best?**

① knew how to liberate it
② learned how to create it
③ figured out how to deliver it
④ understood how to do it

30 **What cannot be inferred from the passage?**

① We have much to learn about how to harness energy from matter.
② Einstein advanced the field of science with his discovery.
③ Ideas we have now in science may one day be proven false as well.
④ We will someday be able to release all the energy stored in matter efficiently.

17 Practice Test

Read the following passages and answer the questions. [01~30] (제한 시간: 45분)

01-03

I think the semicolon is more easily understood if it is defined in relation to the colon rather than to the comma. Under "Semicolon," the book says, "Its main role is to indicate a separation between two parts of a sentence that is stronger than a comma but less strong than dividing the sentence in two with a full stop …. She looked at me; I was lost for words." So the semicolon is exactly what it looks like: a subtle hybrid of colon and comma. Actually, in ancient Greek, the same symbol was used to indicate a question.

And it still seems to have a vestigial interrogative quality to it, a cue to the reader that the writer is not finished yet; she is holding her breath. For example, if the sentence above — "She looked at me; I was lost for words" — occurred as dialogue in a piece that I was copy-editing, I would be tempted to poke in a period and make it into two sentences. In general, people — even people in love — do not speak in flights that demand semicolons. But in this instance I have to admit that without the semicolon something would be lost. With a period, the four words sink at the end: SHE LOOKED at me. The semicolon keeps the words above water: because of that semicolon, something about her look is going to be significant.

01 **What's the idea of the passage?**

① To explain the history of the usage of the semicolon

② To demonstrate the various uses of the semicolon

③ To discuss the need for and effect of semicolons

④ To encourage more usage of semicolons

02 What is the opinion of the writer?

① Semicolons reflect the natural rhythm of spoken English.
② Semicolons add an element of meaning that a period takes away.
③ Semicolons are usually unnecessary in modern languages.
④ It is easy to see why many people regularly misuse semicolons.

03 All of the following are incorrect except ______________________.

① the writer would probably replace a semicolon with a period when copy-editing
② the semicolon was often confused with a question mark in ancient Greece
③ a semicolon implies that there is something important about the first clause mentioned
④ a semicolon has the appearance of a hybrid of a period and a comma

04-05

There may be intangible benefits to being an Olympic city. In 1987, faced with mass protests calling for democracy, South Korea's ruling generals could have given the order to open fire, but that would have ruined the 1988 Seoul Olympics. Instead they gave in to the protesters' demands. The Olympic spotlight thus helped South Korea become a democracy : ______________. That did not, however, work for China, where the 2008 games were accompanied by a political crackdown. As for host countries that already have pluralistic politics, the benefits are not obvious. A study by Stefan Szymanski and Georgios Kavetsos found that hosting a big sporting event makes people significantly happier — so long as that event is the football World Cup. For the Olympics, the "hedonic effect" was insignificant.

04 **Which of the following best fits for the blank?**

① God knows ② no small boon

③ that's outmoded thinking ④ no big deal

05 **Which of the following is incorrect according to the passage?**

① China maintains very strict control over its people.

② The Football World Cup as well as the Olympics can cause people to be happy.

③ Large sporting events can place political spot lights on governments.

④ The people of South Korea were probably very happy that the Olympics came to their country.

06-08

Many Chinese believe that when you marry someone, you are marrying into a lifestyle and an entire family. In a country with conservative marriage traditions, many men and women still think divorce is shameful and that second marriages should be low-profile. China has some long-standing traditions when it comes to marriage, including especially tight family ties, living with the husband's family after marriage, and having the wife serve his parents and potentially his entire family. In modern days, couples who live and work in more westernized urban areas are less likely to abide by such traditions, but they have not completely disappeared and <u>may remain in the back of women's minds like a time bomb</u>. Many single Chinese women therefore find it difficult to decide whom to marry. On the one hand, marrying a relatively rich divorced man is like taking a "secondhand" man, and they may feel they lose face by doing so. On the other hand, marrying an affluent "phoenix man" might embroil the woman in endless troubles with his extended family.

06 Which of the following is true, according to the passage?

① Although divorce is allowed, many Chinese look down on it.
② If a woman doesn't want to get married, she is applauded for her independence.
③ Upon marrying, the husband expects his wife to quit her job to care for the home.
④ A westernized Chinese couple do not have the luxury of choosing their own lifestyle.

07 What's the difference between a "phoenix man" and a "secondhand man"?

① A secondhand man has been divorced; a phoenix man has never married.
② A secondhand man is very wealthy whereas a phoenix man does not have much money.
③ While a secondhand man has had many previous women, a phoenix man has only had one.
④ A secondhand man does not mind getting divorced; however, a phoenix man does not agree with it.

08 What does the underlined mean?

① Career women know that if they do not act in a traditional way when they get married, they will have marital troubles.
② Urban women are dreading the time when they are expected to act like a traditional wife.
③ City women know that the time will come when they have to give up their single life and find a husband.
④ Chinese women push to the back of their minds the thought that marriage will mean the end of their freedom.

09-11

A criminal trial is never about seeking justice for the victim. If it were, there could be only one verdict : guilty. That's because only one person is on trial in a criminal case, and if that one person is acquitted, then by definition there can be no justice for the victim in that trial. A criminal trial is neither a whodunit nor a multiple choice test. It is not even a criminal investigation to determine who among various possible suspects might be responsible for a terrible tragedy. In a murder trial, the state, with all of its power, accuses an individual of being the perpetrator of a dastardly act against a victim. The state must prove that accusation by admissible evidence and beyond a reasonable doubt. Even if it is "likely" or "probable" that a defendant committed the murder, he must be acquitted, because neither likely nor probable satisfies the daunting standard of proof beyond a reasonable doubt. Accordingly, a legally proper result may not be the same as a morally just result. In such a case, justice has not been done to the victim, but the law has prevailed. That is why a criminal trial is not a search for truth. Scientists search for truth. Philosophers search for morality. (A) : proof beyond a reasonable doubt.

09 **What's the passage basically about?**

① The process experienced in a criminal trial
② The real meaning of a criminal trial
③ The optimal resolution of a criminal trial
④ The problems with embarking on a criminal trial

10 **Choose the false statement from the following.**

① Even though a defendant may be found not guilty, the existence of the trial brings justice for the victim.
② A legally sound result is not the same as making sure that the victim feels morally victorious.
③ At the completion of a criminal trial, the perpetrator of the crime may not have been found.
④ Finding the truth behind a crime is not the purpose of undergoing a criminal trial.

11 **Which of the following fits in the blank (　　A　　) best?**

① In what case should a criminal trial be held
② If this is what a criminal trial is looking for
③ When a criminal trial is correctly followed
④ A criminal trial searches for only one result

12–14

It's here that the notion of students teaching teachers is illuminating. As a friend and fellow professor said to me: "You don't just teach students, you have to learn them too." It took a minute — it sounded like he was channeling Huck Finn — but I figured it out. With every class we teach, we need to learn who the people in front of us are. We need to know where they are intellectually, who they are as people and what we can do to help them grow. Teaching, even when you have a group of a hundred students on hand, is a matter of dialogue. In the summer Shakespeare course I'm teaching now, I'm constantly working to figure out what my students are able to do and how they can develop. Can they grasp the contours of Shakespeare's plots? If not, it's worth adding a well-made film version of the next play to the syllabus. Is the language hard for them, line to line? Then we have to spend more time going over individual speeches word by word. Are they adept at understanding the plot and the language? Time to introduce them to the complexities of Shakespeare's rendering of character. Every memorable class is a bit like a jazz composition. There is the basic melody that you work with. It is defined by the syllabus. But there is also a considerable measure of improvisation against that disciplining background.

12 Which of the following is correct, according to the passage?

① A good teacher has all the tools to help students, but none of the personality to get through to them.

② A good teacher teaches each student individually no matter how long it takes.

③ A good teacher gets to know each student individually.

④ A good teacher not only teaches students but learns from them, too.

13 **What is the idea of the passage?**

① Teachers need to put in the legwork and apply themselves to teach their students better.

② Students have much higher expectations of teachers now than in the past.

③ In order for students to learn fully they need to submit themselves to the knowledge and experience of their teachers.

④ An upside-down version of the simple educational premise that students learn from teachers.

14 **What would the professor do if his class did not understand the plot?**

① The professor would make sure each student came to see him individually.

② The professor would show them a modern movie retelling of the story.

③ The professor would go over each part of the story and break down the plot.

④ The professor would get students to act out the play and take on the character roles.

15-17

In 1748, Franklin, then 42 years old, had expanded his printing business throughout the colonies and become successful enough to stop working. Retirement allowed him to concentrate on public service and also pursue more fully his longtime interest in science. In the 1740s, he conducted experiments that contributed to the understanding of electricity, and invented the lightning rod, which protected buildings from fires caused by lightning. In 1752, he conducted his famous kite experiment and demonstrated that lightning is electricity. <u>Franklin also coined a number of electricity-related terms</u>, including battery, charge and conductor. In addition to electricity, Franklin studied a number of other topics, including ocean currents, meteorology, causes of the common cold and refrigeration. He developed the Franklin stove, which provided more heat while using less fuel than other stoves, and bifocal eyeglasses, which allow for distance and reading use. In the early 1760s, Franklin invented a musical instrument called the glass armonica. Composers such as Ludwig Beethoven (1770-1827) and Wolfgang Mozart (1756-91) wrote music for Franklin's armonica; however, by the early part of the 19th century, the once-popular instrument had largely fallen out of use.

15 **How was Franklin able to spend time on inventing?**

① He was given sufficient money from sponsors who believed in him.
② He did not like his job and rushed home to continue inventing.
③ He had earned enough money to not need to work anymore.
④ He did not have any family to take care of, so he had a lot of free time.

16 Which of the following is false, according to the passage?

① The armonica is no longer a popular instrument and has not been for a long time.

② Franklin was responsible for the popularity of the battery.

③ He managed to invent a stove that used less fuel but produced more heat.

④ The kite experiment showed that lightning was actually electricity.

17 Which of the following paraphrases the underlined?

① Franklin put lots of money into his business to make items that transmitted electricity.

② Franklin came to terms with that he had done in the field of electricity.

③ Franklin made up words that would describe things associated with electricity.

④ Franklin was not good at finding ways to describe electricity.

18-20

Perhaps the most pulse-quickening topic of all is "conditional probability" — the probability that some event A happens, given (or "conditional" upon) the occurrence of some other event B. It's a slippery concept, easily conflated with the probability of B given A. They're not the same, but you have to concentrate to see why. For example, consider the following word problem.

Before going on vacation for a week, you ask your spacey friend to water your ailing plant. Without water, the plant has a 90 percent chance of dying. Even with proper watering, it has a 20 percent chance of dying. And the probability that your friend will forget to water it is 30 percent. (a) What's the chance that your plant will survive the week? (b) If it's dead when you return, what's the chance that your friend forgot to water it? (c) If your friend forgot to water it, what's the chance it'll be dead when you return? Although they sound alike, (b) and (c) are not the same. In fact, the problem tells us that the answer to (c) is 90 percent. But how do you combine all the probabilities to get the answer to (b)? Or (a)?

Naturally, the first few semesters I taught this topic, I stuck to the book, inching along, playing it safe. But gradually I began to notice something. A few of my students would avoid using "Bayes's theorem," the labyrinthine formula I was teaching them. Instead they would solve the problems by a much easier method. What these resourceful students kept discovering, year after year, was a better way to think about conditional probability. Their way comports with human intuition instead of confounding it. The trick is to think in terms of "natural frequencies" — simple counts of events — rather than the more abstract notions of percentages, odds, or probabilities. ______________________________

18 Which of the following best fits for the blank?

① As soon as you make this mental shift, the fog lifts.
② Changing your way of thinking cannot teach you everything.
③ When you have understood something, you feel lighter.
④ Having mental strength will make the idea clearer.

19 What can be inferred from the passage?

① The majority of students find the concept easy from the outset, while a few struggle.
② The writer finds the teaching of this topic tedious.
③ Conditional probability is a difficult concept to grasp, even for those who study the field.
④ Understanding Bayes's theorem is not important to understand conditional probability.

20 What's the benefit of the students' method, according to the passage?

① The students can pass on their experience year after year to new students.
② Their way of thinking works in parallel with natural human thought rather than against it.
③ They learn enough to be able to understand it, but not enough to become bored by it.
④ The students' method has much less to do with Bayes's theorem.

21-23

Researching how people's unconscious assumptions affect their perception of economic issues, I explored the linguistic dynamics behind the term "middle class," especially in comparison to other economic groupings. In the Corpus of Contemporary American English, a database of more than 450 million words from speeches, media, fiction, and academic texts, among the most common words (excluding conjunctions and prepositions among others) co-occurring with "middle class" we find "emerging," "burgeoning," "burdened," and "squeezed." These tell us what happens to this grouping. Absent are quantitative terms or descriptors for what life is like within this category. In fact, in common usage, we rarely hear about actual people named within it; middle class may as well describe a grouping of potted plants or pop cans. There's little here tied to income or lifestyle.

Conversely, statements about "the wealthy" co-occur with terms like "investors," "businessmen," "patrons," "owners," and "donors." What these words indicate is a sense of sources of income and, by extension, the amount compensated. The wealthy, in our language, aren't acted upon but rather act as human members of a group who get things done and pay themselves to do it.

"Poor," once the meaning of low quality is filtered out, comes with "guy" and "girl" but also "homeless," "sick," "plight," "needy," and "suffering." Those descriptors provide a sense what it's like to be in this group day to day, and they make pretty clear it's made up of people who aren't allowed any or much income.

Poking into usage also confirms that Americans are relatively skittish about mentioning class. Contrasting databases of text from U.S. and UK sources, we find that Brits use "upper class" and "lower class" more readily; we prefer "wealthy" and "poor." Yet we grant "middle class" plenty of airtime. This suggests it's a frozen phrase, no longer rooted in the meaning of component parts that ought to designate economic status between two others. Instead, middle class has become a status, a brand — ______________________.

21 **Which phrase best completes the sentence?**

① something that can be purchased
② that everyone shies away from
③ a label you opt to adopt
④ with all the connotations that go along with it

22 **What can be inferred from the passage?**

① Americans don't see "middle class" as being intrinsically linked with how much money you have.
② Americans feel the word "class" is the only suitable one to talk about the rich and the poor.
③ When rich people are being discussed, it is vulgar to use the word "upper class" to describe them.
④ The class system is alive and strong in America and coming more into use.

23 **Which is true about the term "middle class"?**

① It is used more commonly in the UK than it is in the US.
② It is the most commonly used of all the class terms because it has little meaning.
③ Americans never use the term as it is too judgmental for their tastes.
④ The term is not used with any indication of the people and lives it is describing.

24-27

South Korea, a country where until recently people were taught to take pride in their nation's "ethnic homogeneity" and where the words "skin color" and "peach" are synonymous, is struggling to embrace a new reality. In just the past seven years, the number of foreign residents has doubled, to 1.2 million, even as the country's population of 48.7 million is expected to drop sharply in coming decades because of its low birth rate.

Many of the foreigners come here to toil at sea or on farms or in factories, providing cheap labor in jobs shunned by South Koreans. Southeast Asian women marry rural farmers who cannot find South Korean brides. People from English-speaking countries find jobs teaching English in a society obsessed with learning the language from native speakers.

For most South Koreans, globalization has largely meant increasing exports or going abroad to study. But now that it is also bringing an influx of foreigners into a society where 42 percent of respondents in a 2008 survey said they had never once spoken with a foreigner, South Koreans are learning to adjust — often uncomfortably.

In a report issued last year, Amnesty International criticized discrimination in South Korea against migrant workers, who mostly are from poor Asian countries, citing sexual abuse, racial slurs, inadequate safety training and the mandatory disclosure of H.I.V. status, a requirement not imposed on South Koreans in the same jobs. Citing local news media and rights advocates, it said that following last year's financial downturn, "incidents of xenophobia are on the rise."

24 What's the passage about?

① The frequency with which foreigners are now entering South Korea.
② The adjustments that foreigners have to make when coming to South Korea.
③ Tensions as a result of an increased foreign population in South Korea.
④ The societal problems that arise when foreigners do not get on well in South Korea.

25 What kind of paragraph best follows this passage?

① The amount of money spent on English-language education in South Korea per annum.
② Other countries around the world where Southeast Asians are treated poorly.
③ The different news media outlets that protect foreigners and those that accuse them of wrongdoing.
④ Some examples where South Koreans have shown xenophobic sentiments to foreigners.

26 Which of the following is correct, according to the passage?

① As the population of ethnic Koreans falls, the numbers of foreigners in South Korea rises.
② Even now, less than half of South Koreans had spoken to a foreigner.
③ Migrant workers and South Koreans who work in factories are subject to the same stringent rules.
④ The concept of globalization in South Korea has changed from export to import.

27 Why is a cosmopolitan society hard for South Koreans to adjust to, according to the passage?

① Foreigners are not coming to South Korea in as strong numbers as they used to.
② They have been raised to applaud the fact that their society is ethnically identical.
③ South Koreans do not understand the language or the culture of foreigners.
④ The birth rate in South Korea is negatively affected by foreigners joining the population.

28-30

The truth is made worse by the reality that no one — really no one — anywhere on the political spectrum has the courage to speak out about the madness of unleashed guns and what they do to American life. That includes the President, whose consoling message managed to avoid the issue of why these killings take place. Of course, we don't know, and perhaps never will, what exactly "made him" do what he did; but we know how he did it. Those who fight for the right of every madman and every criminal to have as many people-killing weapons as they want share moral responsibility for what happened recently — as they will when it happens again. And it will happen again.

The reality is simple: every country struggles with madmen and ideologues with guns, and every country — Canada, Norway, Britain — has had a gun massacre once, or twice. Then people act to stop them, and they do — as over the past few years has happened in Australia. Only in America are gun massacres of this kind routine, expectable, and certain to continue. Does anyone even remember any longer a lot of massacres?

But nothing changes: the blood lobby still blares out its certainties, including the pretense that the Second Amendment — despite the clear grammar of its first sentence — is designed not to protect citizen militias but to make sure that no lunatic goes unarmed. Make sure that guns designed for no reason save to kill people are freely available to anyone who wants one — and that is, and remains, the essential American condition — and then be shocked when children are killed. For all the good work the Brady Campaign to Prevent Gun Violence tries to do, nothing changes.

28 What is NOT an opinion of the passage?

① Those who say every American should have a gun are partly guilty when a tragedy occurs.

② Giving a gun to every American means both the sane and the insane get to have one.

③ The ease of getting guns in America causes gun crime.

④ People in America have had enough of senseless gun crime and are demanding change.

29 Which of the following can you infer?

① Americans are shocked when a tragedy occurs and demand change, but the government refuses to listen.

② The people who think it is okay for anyone to have a gun are fully aware of their role in certain tragedies.

③ Speaking out against the right of anyone to have a gun would certainly have a negative effect on a politician's career.

④ The Second Amendment is misunderstood by those on both sides of the argument over guns.

30 Which of the following correctly paraphrases the underlined phrase?

① It is important that the guns which serve no purpose other than killing are readily available.

② Suppose that your gun has nothing to offer you apart from killing someone, would you keep it?

③ People should be free to choose whichever kind of gun they want, even if that gun can kill people.

④ Those who want a gun for killing need to make sure that they purchase the right gun for that situation.

18 Practice Test

Read the following passages and answer the questions. [01~30] (제한 시간: 45분)

01–03

Most marketing conventions will tell you that it's important to establish your brand and to get people familiar with your products and services. A different marketing technique is also available at your disposal and it certainly has both its strengths and its weaknesses. I'm talking about the teaser.

On television, you may have noticed some commercials that don't seem to feature the target product at all. In fact, there may not be any explicit mention of the company behind the ad. It may be comprised of some random event or a story that begins but stops part way through. Typically, at the end of these "teaser" ads, you are either presented with a teaser statement of some kind or with a nondescript URL to a website.

With the former, the goal is to create a viral marketing campaign. They want to get people talking about that ad so that they can discuss what the ad could be all about. More people will talk about it, more interest will be generated, and people will be anxious to find out what is the true nature of that ad. It's hard to get people interested in an ad campaign, and a "teaser" strategy just might work.

If the teaser ad ends with the prominently displaying of a URL, people may feel more inclined to visit the website compared to a conventional ad that ends with a URL. People will be motivated to go to the website to find out more about what the teaser was really trying to show. Naturally, the biggest downside to this strategy is that if the person does not go to the website, they may never be motivated enough to find out the nature of the ad and, thus, your marketing dollars may go to waste.

01 **Which of the following is the best title for the passage?**

① Advertising differences
② A new approach to ads
③ The quickest ads
④ Teaser advertising

02 **What can be inferred from the passage?**

① Companies put a lot of effort into designing teaser ads that will attract people's attention.
② There are very few companies that will risk spending money on teaser ads.
③ There are limited ways that companies can advertise something to people.
④ Teaser ads work best when used in areas where people have access to the internet.

03 **What is the main purpose of the passage?**

① To explain why companies use teasers sometimes instead of regular advertisements.
② To show the different types of ads that can be used by companies.
③ To show the up and down side to using certain kinds of advertisements.
④ To explain the two types to advertisements that can be used for selling a product.

04-07

Some conscientious objectors are unwilling to serve the military in any capacity, while others accept noncombatant roles. While conscientious objection is usually the refusal to collaborate with military organizations, as a combatant in war or in any supportive role, some advocate compromising forms of conscientious objection. One compromising form is to accept non-combatant roles during conscription or military service. Alternatives to military or civilian service include serving an imprisonment or other punishment for refusing conscription, falsely claiming unfitness for duty by feigning an allergy or a heart condition, delaying conscription until the maximum drafting age, or seeking refuge in a country which does not extradite those wanted for military conscription. Avoiding military service is sometimes labeled draft dodging, particularly if the goal is accomplished through dishonesty or evasive maneuvers. However, many people who support conscription will distinguish between "bona fide" conscientious objection and draft dodging, which they view as evasion of military service without a valid excuse.

Conscientious objection exists since the incorporation of forced military service but was not officially recognized until the twentieth century, when it was gradually recognized as a fundamental human right as a part of the freedom of conscience. Despite the fact that international institutions like the United Nations (UN) or the Council of Europe (CoE) regard and promote conscientious objection as a human right, as of 2004, it still does not have a legal basis in most countries. Among the roughly one-hundred countries that have conscription, only thirty countries have some legal provisions, 25 of them in Europe. In Europe, most countries with conscription more or less fulfill international guidelines on conscientious objection legislation (except for Greece, Cyprus, Turkey, Finland and Russia) today. In many countries outside Europe, especially in armed conflict areas (Israel, Democratic Republic of the Congo), conscientious objection is punished severely.

04 **What can be inferred from the passage?**

① The laws in some countries are more archaic than in others.
② There are a lot of people around the world who don't believe the righteousness of the war.
③ There is no end to the amount of violence being done in areas like Israel.
④ Every country in the world would use conscription if they could.

05 **Which of the following is incorrect according to the passage?**

① Conscription is a way of adding members to the military.
② Most countries do not have strict laws protecting conscious objectors.
③ Some countries allow objectors to work in non-combative roles.
④ To object to doing what your country wants you to do is illegal.

06 **What is the main topic of the passage?**

① People choosing to not kill others in the name of their country
② The different policies countries have in regard to their military recruitment.
③ How to avoid military service
④ Why people try to avoid military service through illegal means.

07 **What is the meaning of the underlined phrase?**

① To refuse because one's conscious tells them it is wrong
② To object internally
③ To disagree with what others are doing no matter what the reason
④ To have an objectionable understanding of something

08-09

The bestselling coauthor of *Raising Cain*, hailed for its insights into the psyche of boys, breaks new ground with this startling picture of today's American girl — independent, self-confident, highly motivated, and fundamentally different from previous generations.

There's a new type of teenage girl growing up in America today, and she is having a profound and beneficial influence on society. That's the conclusion of Dr. Dan Kindlon, the widely respected child and adolescent psychologist and the coauthor of the bestseller *Raising Cain*. Dr. Kindlon supports his startling discoveries about the "alpha girl" with groundbreaking research, including profiles, case studies, questionnaires and more. In Alpha Girls, Dr. Kindlon: ① Presents innovative, newsworthy material about teenage girls that directly contradicts the thesis of *Reviving Ophelia*. ② Looks at the many ways in which the accomplishments of the alpha girl's mother have helped to liberate her daughter. ③ Examines the dramatically different relationship today between father and daughter — and how it can transform a girl's psychological makeup, identity, and sense of self.

Part of the first generation that is reaping the full benefits of the women's movement, today's American girl is maturing with a new sense of possibility and psychological emancipation. Dr. Kindlon provides us with an in-depth portrait of the alpha girl — a born leader who is ready to explode into adulthood and make her mark on the world and, by her example serve as an inspiration for women everywhere.

08 What can be inferred from the passage?

① Teenage girls are much more independent and self-confident than they used to be.

② There are many new psychological problems developing because of the freedom girls have now.

③ Defiant girls are making it a much more difficult for boys to do well.

④ There are new opportunities for teenage girls as they continue to mature mentally.

09 Which of the following is correct according to the passage?

① Girls have become dominate over boys their same age.

② The alpha girl is much more of a leader than boys.

③ The women's movement has taken until now to allow girls to fully benefit from its work.

④ The psyche of alpha girls is identical to that of regular boys.

10-12

ENGEL'S LAW: As incomes rise the percentage of total income spent on basic food and other necessities declines. Engel's Law does not say the amount spent on necessities declines — 5% of a $50,000 salary ($2,500) spent on food is more than 20% of a $5,000 salary ($1,000), or 40% of a $500 salary ($200). In poor countries people spend, on average, 35% to 40% of their very small incomes on food — mostly basic raw food items such as beans, potatoes, corn, rice, etc. In middle-income countries the average spent is about 10% to 15% of their somewhat higher income on basic raw food items. In rich countries basic food accounts for only 1% to 4% of total spending. Obviously we spend much more than 1 to 4 % of our incomes at the grocery store and in restaurants, but most of that spending is for other than basic food items. Of course, the 1% of the very high incomes in rich countries is much more in absolute terms than the 15% spent on food in middle-income countries, and many times greater than the 40% spent on food in poor countries.

Engel's Law is law; it is true for all people, in all countries, at all times in the past, and will be true for everyone in the future. Engel's Law is true because it correctly describes human behavior. One cannot hold Engel's law to be false, (A) one can suppose people would prefer to spend their money on things they don't want rather than spend it on those things they do want. The elasticity of demand for food and other necessities is low relative to the elasticity of demand for manufactured products and services. As we increase our consumption of food, and those other commodities that we consider necessities, our desire for consuming even more declines rapidly — we say demand for those commodities is inelastic. In the early stages of development, people may shift their diet from corn and beans to meat and other more costly foods. But, even in this case they would be shifting from necessities that keep them alive, to luxury foods that they prefer. At some point people find it unnecessary to "improve" their diets, and prefer to spend most of their extra money on manufactured goods and services.

10 Which of the following means the same as the underlined phrase?

① The amount that the demand for a product can be extended over time.

② The amount of increase or decrease in desire or need for something.

③ The amount of people that want the same thing at the same time.

④ The value people place on necessities they want to have.

11 Which of the following word or phrase best fit the blank (A)?

① until

② but also

③ so much as

④ any more than

12 What is the main purpose of the passage?

① To show how people of all economic levels spend the same amount.

② To explain how Engel's law can apply similarly to people of different economic backgrounds.

③ To show how necessity is the driving force behind the purchase of necessities.

④ To explain why people need to spend money on both necessary and wanted items.

13-15

An AMBER Alert is a child abduction alert bulletin in several countries throughout the world, issued upon the suspected abduction of a child, since 1996. AMBER is officially an acronym for "America's Missing: Broadcasting Emergency Response" but was originally named for Amber Hagerman, a 9-year-old child who was abducted and murdered in Arlington, Texas in 1996.

AMBER Alerts are distributed via commercial radio stations, satellite radio, television stations, and cable TV by the Emergency Alert System and NOAA Weather Radio (where they are termed "Child Abduction Emergency" or "Amber Alerts"). The alerts are also issued via e-mail, electronic trafficcondition signs, the LED billboards which are located outside of newer Walgreens locations, along with the LED/LCD signs of billboard companies such as Clear Channel Outdoor, CBS Outdoor and Lamar, or through wireless device SMS text messages.

Those interested in subscribing to receive AMBER Alerts in their area via SMS messages can visit Wireless Amber Alerts, which are offered by law as free messages. In some states, the display scrollboards in front of lottery terminals are also used. The decision to declare an AMBER Alert is made by each police organization (in many cases, the State Police or Highway Patrol) which investigates each of the abductions. Public information in an AMBER Alert usually consists of the name and description of the abductee, a description of the suspected abductor, and a description and license plate number of the abductor's vehicle, (A).

13 What can be inferred from the passage?

① The police have a high success rate at finding abductees using AMBER alerts.
② There are not many other ways to find missing children.
③ Most people pay close attention Amber alerts trying to help as much as possible.
④ Abductions occur frequently making the alert system a valuable and necessary tool.

14 What is the best title for the passage?

① How Amber helps children.
② The problem of abduction.
③ The AMBER method.
④ The best way to find lost children.

15 Which of the following word or phrase best fit the blank (A)?

① if any
② as soon as possible
③ if available
④ against all odds

16–18

Project financing is an innovative and timely financing technique that has been used on many high-profile corporate projects, including Euro Disneyland and the Eurotunnel. Employing a carefully engineered financing mix, it has long been used to fund large-scale natural resource projects, from pipelines and refineries to electric-generating facilities and hydro-electric projects. Increasingly, project financing is emerging as the preferred alternative to conventional methods of financing infrastructure and other large-scale projects worldwide.

Project Financing discipline includes understanding the rationale for project financing, how to prepare the financial plan, assess the risks, design the financing mix, and raise the funds. In addition, one must understand the cogent analyses of why some project financing plans have succeeded while others have failed. A knowledge-base is required regarding the design of contractual arrangements to support project financing; issues for the host government legislative provisions, public/private infrastructure partnerships, public/private financing structures; credit requirements of lenders, and how to determine the project's borrowing capacity; how to prepare cash flow projections and use them to measure expected rates of return; tax and accounting considerations; and analytical techniques to validate the project's feasibility.

Project finance is finance for a particular project, such as a mine, toll road, railway, pipeline, power station, ship, hospital or prison, which is repaid from the cash-flow of that project. Project finance is different from traditional forms of finance because the financier principally looks to the assets and revenue of the project in order to secure and service the loan. In contrast to an ordinary borrowing situation, in a project financing the financier usually has little or no recourse to the non-project assets of the borrower or the sponsors of the project. In this situation, the credit risk associated with the borrower is not as important as in an ordinary loan transaction; what is most important is the identification, analysis, allocation and management of every risk associated with the project.

16 What can be inferred from the passage?

① There are many risks involved when starting any project of any size.
② There are only a few companies that can afford to develop this type of project.
③ This type of project financing can ruin a company if things do not go according to plan.
④ The repayment of a project finance loan is very much dependant on variables outside the control of either party involved.

17 Which of the following is incorrect according to the passage?

① Project financing is a last resort for a company to complete a project.
② Project financing is a complicated process.
③ There are a lot of financing figures to account for when developing the financing for a project.
④ Project financing is usually done for large and expensive construction projects.

18 Which of the following is the purpose of the second paragraph?

① To tell the reader what to prepare for their project.
② To show why many projects fail from a lack of preparedness.
③ To illustrate the complexity of the planning required in project financing.
④ To explain why the planning process is central to any project of a large scale.

19-21

Parkinson's Law is the adage first articulated by Cyril Northcote Parkinson as the first sentence of a humorous essay published in The Economist in 1955. "Work expands so as to fill the time available for its completion." It was later reprinted together with other essays in the book Parkinson's Law: The Pursuit of Progress (London, John Murray, 1958). He derived the dictum from his extensive experience in the British Civil Service.

The current form of the law is not that which Parkinson refers to by that name in the article. Rather, he assigns to the term a mathematical equation describing the rate at which bureaucracies expand over time. Much of the essay is dedicated to a summary of purportedly scientific observations supporting his law, such as the increase in the number of employees at the Colonial Office while Great Britain's overseas empire declined (indeed, he shows that the Colonial Office had its greatest number of staff at the point when it was folded into the Foreign Office because of a lack of colonies to administer). He explains this growth by two forces: (1) "An official wants to multiply subordinates, not rivals" and (2) "Officials make work for each other." He notes in particular that the total of those employed inside a bureaucracy rose by 5-7% per year "irrespective of any variation in the amount of work (if any) to be done."

19 What is meant by the underlined phrase?

① The more time given to complete a job the more time is used to complete that task.

② Work is always more complicated than it originally seems.

③ There is never enough time given by superiors to complete a job.

④ The faster work is done the more work is given to the employees that complete it.

20 What can be inferred about bureaucracies from the passage?

① They are one of the most efficient ways of organizing a large government.

② They have a great understanding of the inner workings of their government.

③ They are not the most efficient offices.

④ They are over worked.

21 Which of the following is not correct according to the passage?

① Only the British Empire ever followed this law.

② Parkinson's Law has evolved from its original form.

③ Bureaucratic officers make work for each other.

④ With time governments tend to expand at the bureaucratic level.

22-24

In 1991, Anita Hill stepped into the glare of the national spotlight, testifying before the all-male Senate Judiciary Committee about the vulgar sexual advances she said she endured a decade earlier while working at two government agencies for Clarence Thomas, the nominee to the Supreme Court. Those hearings brought into the open the problem of sexual harassment — <u>an issue that millions of women privately recognized but rarely discussed</u>. For many, having a way to define and label the behavior was empowering.

In the months and years afterward, recognition of the issue grew and tolerance of harassment in workplaces and on campuses shrank. The law changed, too. The month after the hearings, Congress passed a law that allowed sexual harassment victims to seek damage awards as well as back pay and reinstatement. It was signed by President George H. W. Bush, who had threatened to veto the act just a week before Ms. Hill testified.

Initial fears that Ms. Hill's shoddy treatment by the Judiciary Committee would deter victims of sexual harassment from coming forward proved unfounded. The Equal Employment Opportunity Commission, where Ms. Hill worked for Mr. Thomas during his time as its chairman, saw a 50 percent increase in sexual harassment filings the year after the hearing. In the 2010 fiscal year, according to the commission, the number of such filings with the E.E.O.C. and state and local fair employment agencies totaled 11,717, compared with 6,883 in 1991.

In the past three decades, many companies have started training programs to deter sexual harassment. But even with greater employer attention, only a small fraction of harassment victims risk stigma and potential job loss to pursue claims. While much work remains, Ms. Hill's courage opened the way for meaningful progress against this form of sex-discrimination. It is a legacy worth celebrating.

22 **What can be inferred from the passage?**

① George Bush is a strong supporter of women's rights.
② Sexual harassment is still a big issue for the United States to deal with.
③ There are many companies that no longer allow any sexual harassment.
④ The definition of sexual harassment has changed over time.

23 **Which of the following mean the same as the underlined?**

① A lot of women experience and deal with sexual harassment, but few tell anyone about it.
② Many women hear about sexual harassment, but no one really talks about it.
③ Many women never have it happen to them so they don't talk about it.
④ The vast majority of women do not consider what happens to them sexual harassment.

24 **What is the conclusion the writer comes to about the issue of sexual harassment?**

① Ms. Hill has left a legacy for women to celebrate.
② Things are going in the right direction, but much more has yet to be done.
③ There are many more women suffering sexual harassment.
④ The struggle against sexual harassment is drawing to a close.

25-28

The term "plastic surgery" originates from the Greek word "plastikos," which means to mold or shape. The field of Plastic Surgery can be broken down into two main categories—reconstructive procedures and cosmetic procedures. Both are generally considered sub-specialties of plastic surgery.

Reconstructive surgery is performed to restore function and normal appearance, and correct deformities created by birth defects, trauma or medical conditions including cancer. Examples include cleft lip and palate repair, breast reconstruction following a lumpectomy or mastectomy for breast cancer, and reconstructive surgery after burn injuries. Typically, reconstructive surgery is considered medically necessary and is covered by most health insurance plans. Cosmetic surgery is performed to enhance overall cosmetic appearance by reshaping and adjusting normal anatomy to make it visually more appealing. Unlike reconstructive surgery, cosmetic surgery is not considered medically necessary. Breast augmentation, breast lift, liposuction, abdominoplasty (tummy tuck) and facelift are popular examples of cosmetic surgery procedures.

In reality, there is often significant overlap between reconstructive and cosmetic plastic surgery since they share many of the same underlying surgical principles. No matter the type of plastic surgery that is being performed, the end goal should always include maximizing the cosmetic result as much as possible. Regardless of the plastic surgery procedure being planned, it is very important for patients to discuss the anticipated cosmetic result with their surgeon ____________________.

The lines between reconstructive and cosmetic surgery are further blurred when it comes to insurance coverage. Certain conditions can be deemed either "reconstructive" or "cosmetic" depending on the patient's specific situation. A perfect example is rhinoplasty (nose surgery) which is often performed to enhance the appearance of the nose but may also be required to restore normal nasal breathing and normal appearance after a bad nasal fracture.

25 **What is the passage mainly about?**

① The dominance of cosmetic surgery over reconstructive in the medical community.
② Reasons why insurance covers reconstructive surgery but not that of cosmetic.
③ The necessity of plastic surgery to improve people's lives.
④ Similarities and differences between reconstructive and cosmetic surgery.

26 **What can be inferred about plastic surgery?**

① Those born with physical abnormalities are given access to the best surgeons.
② Many reconstructive surgeries are labeled incorrectly as cosmetic.
③ Plastic surgeons choose their profession because they are not as skilled as regular doctors.
④ People elect to undergo surgery for different reasons, but the end goal is the same.

27 **According to the passage, which of the following is false?**

① Patients are more likely to want to change their breasts, lips, or stomachs.
② Both cosmetic and reconstructive surgeries have a better appearance as their objective.
③ Reconstructive surgery is often sought after by people dissatisfied with their appearance.
④ Reconstructive surgery is performed on those who have suffered physical problems.

28 **Which best completes the sentence?**

① ahead of time to ensure appropriate expectations are met
② in order to make sure they are making the right decision
③ to guarantee more surgeries are not needed in the future
④ so that the correct post-surgery care will be administered

29-30

When your favorite sports team won the national championship last year, did you make a point of wearing the team cap? And when your best friend won that special award, do you remember how often you told others the good news about your friend? If you played a role in someone's success, it's understandable that you would want to share in the recognition however, people often want to share recognition even when they are on the sidelines of an outstanding achievement. Basking in reflected glory is the tendency to enhance one's image by publicly announcing one's association with those who are successful.

Robert Cialdini and his colleagues studied this phenomenon on college campuses with nationally ranked football teams. They predicted that, when asked how their team had fared in a recent football game, students would be more likely to say, "We won" (in other words, to bask in reflected glory, or to "BIRG") when the home team had been successful than to respond "We lost" when it had been defeated. As predicted, students were more likely to BIRG when their team won than when it lost. Also, subjects who believed that they had just failed a bogus test were more likely to use the words "we won" than those who believed they had performed well. A related self-enhancement strategy is "CORFing," or cutting off reflected failure. Because self-esteem is partly tied to an individual's associations with others, people often protect their self-esteem by distancing themselves from those who are unsuccessful. Thus, if your cousin is arrested for drunk driving, you may tell others that you and he don't really know each other that well.

29 **What can be inferred from the passage?**

① There are always different ways of attaining lasting glory.
② We like to feel good about ourselves through the admiration of others.
③ Everyone loves to bask in the glory of others.
④ We only bask in the glory of others while we have none of our own.

30 **Which of the following is incorrect according to the passage?**

① Students who do poorly on exams do not want to experience BIRG as much as others.
② People distance themselves from those without glory, or having failure.
③ Failure can be transferred to a person by association.
④ People who are feeling emotionally low use BIRG to lift themselves up.

19 Practice Test

Read the following passages and answer the questions. [01~30] (제한 시간: 45분)

01-03

As the Chinese economy surges, so does interest in Mandarin. The Chinese government estimates some 40m people study Mandarin outside the country, up from 30m in 2005. A tight job market in the West is partly responsible. According to a survey in September by Rosetta Stone, 58% of Americans believe the lack of foreign-language skills among native workers will lead to foreigners taking high-paying jobs. "The recession has focused people on where growth is going to come from," says Tom Adams, the firm's chief executive. Among existing corporate customers logging into the company's multi-language programme, the number learning Mandarin increased by 1,800% between 2008 and 2010.

The question remains whether the Mandarin rush will prove a fad. Japanese and Russian also had "hot" periods, only to recede in popularity. And Chinese can be controversial. With some parents fearful of communist influence, a California school district recently turned down $30,000 per year from the Chinese government to pay for Mandarin classes. Yet Mandarin ought to continue to grow. In America just 4% of schools teach the language. In Britain, though Mandarin is spreading, the most popular languages by far remain Spanish, French and German. <u>There is a long way to go before China's main language becomes as widespread as its economic influence</u>.

01 **What's the idea of the passage?**

① Learning Mandarin can increase your ability to communicate globally.
② Learning Mandarin is important for those people who want to climb the corporate ladder.
③ The growth of Mandarin study can be linked to the global economic recession.
④ Many companies are encouraging their employees to learn Mandarin.

02 **What does the underlined sentence mean?**

① China has pushed Mandarin forward as a way to bolster its grip on the global economy.
② Making China a global economy and Mandarin a global language has been a long time coming.
③ As the influence of Mandarin grows more extensive, so the Chinese economy will continue to benefit.
④ It cannot be said that Mandarin is close to becoming as influential as the Chinese economy.

03 **What can be inferred from the passage?**

① Americans are learning Mandarin in order to compete in a tighter job market.
② The number of people learning Mandarin is now rivaling other popular foreign languages.
③ The learning of Mandarin is simply a flash in the pan that will be all but forgotten next year.
④ If you have a second language, you can get a job during these times of recession.

04-06

An essayist is not a mighty traveler. He does not run to grapple with a roaring lion. He desires neither typhoon nor tempest. He is content in his harbor to listen to the storm upon the rocks, if now and then by a lucky chance he can shelter someone from the wreck. His hands are not red with revolt against the world. He has glanced upon the thoughts of many men, and as opposite philosophies point upon the truth, he is modest with his own and tolerant of others. He looks at the stars and, knowing in what a dim immensity we travel, he writes of little things beyond dispute. There are enough to weep upon the shadows; he, like a dial, marks the light. The small clatter of the city beneath his window, the cry of peddlers, children chalking their games upon the pavement, laundry dancing on the roofs, and smoke in the winter's wind — <u>these are the things he weaves into the fabric of his thoughts</u>. Or sheep upon the hillside, if his window is so lucky, or a sunny meadow is a profitable speculation. And so, while the novelist is struggling up a dizzy mountain, straining through the tempest to see the kingdoms of the world, behold the essayist, snug at home, content with little sights! He is a kind of poet — a poet whose wings are clipped. He flaps to no great heights, and sees neither the devil nor the seven oceans nor the twelve apostles. He paints old thoughts in shiny varnish and, as he is able, he mends small habits here and there.

04 What is the main topic of the passage?

① The life of an essayist
② The similarities of writing forms
③ The writing of essays
④ Why essays are boring.

05 Which of the following is the same in meaning as the underlined?

① This is what he thinks about all the time.
② This is what he incorporates into his ideas so as to fit together as one.
③ That is the way he gains inspiration for his work.
④ What he does to help him think of what to write.

06 What is an essayist according to the passage?

① A writer who isn't quite good enough to write novels.
② An unimaginative poet
③ An individual who is afraid to risk going out into the world to gain a new perspective for their writing.
④ A person content to write about the many simple things they see around them.

07-08

My aim is to present a conception of justice which generalizes and carries to a higher level of abstraction the familiar theory of the social contract as found, say, in Locke, Rousseau, and Kant. In order to do this we are not to think of the original contract as one to enter a particular society or to set up a particular form of government. Rather, the guiding idea is that the principles of justice for the basic structure of society are the object of the original agreement. They are the principles that free and rational persons concerned to further their own interests would accept in an initial position of equality as defining the fundamental terms of their association. These principles are to regulate all further agreements; they specify the kinds of social cooperation that can be entered into and the forms of government that can be established. This way of regarding the principles of justice I shall call justice as fairness.

07 **Why would people accept the principles as an initial position according to the passage?**

① The principles are sound and fair to all.

② There are few who could dispute the validity of the principles in question.

③ They allow all those involved to further their own interests in a fair way to all.

④ The principles allow all involved to be regulated by the same set of rules.

08 **What is the main idea of the passage?**

① The use of justice instills a level of fairness in all matters within a society.

② The use of principles to determine the fairness of a position is essential to all.

③ Entering into an agreement must also mean entering into a just and fair social contract.

④ Social contracts require a level of justice for all to ensure fairness.

09–10

The parents' love of the child is expressed in their evident intention to care for him, to do for him as his rational self-love would incline, and in the fulfillment of these intentions. Their love is displayed by their taking pleasure in his presence and supporting his sense of competence and self-esteem. They encourage his efforts to master the tasks of growing up and they welcome his assuming his own place. In general, to love another means not only to be concerned for his wants and needs, but to affirm his sense of the worth of his own person. Eventually, then, the love of the parents for the child gives rise to his love in return. The child's love does not have a rational instrumental explanation: he does not love them as a means to achieve his initial self-interested ends. With this aim in view he could conceivably act as if he loved them, but his doing so would not constitute a transformation of his original desires. By the stated psychological principle, a new affection is in time called into being by the evident love of the parents.

09 What does the passage consider love for another to be?

① To be inclined to be near the person and to want to increase their sense of self worth/esteem

② To have affection for another person

③ To want to fulfill the intentions and desires of another

④ To be part of something bigger than yourself

10 What cannot be inferred from the passage?

① Parents will love their children before children love their parents.

② Love is not something that comes easily to many people.

③ Self love is the most important form of love there is.

④ Love for another requires sacrifice and dedication.

11-13

Half of a typical family's spending today goes to transportation and housing, according to the latest Consumer Expenditure Survey, released by the Bureau of Labor Statistics. At the height of the housing bubble, residential construction and related activities accounted for more than a quarter of the economy in metro areas like Las Vegas and Orlando. Nation new-car and new-truck purchases hovered near historic highs. But Millennials have turned against both cars and houses in dramatic and historic fashion. Just as car sales have plummeted among their age cohort, the share of young people getting their first mortgage between 2009 and 2011 is half what it was just 10 years ago, according to a Federal Reserve study.

Needless to say, the Great Recession is responsible for some of the decline. But it's highly possible that <u>a perfect storm of economic and demographic factors</u> — from high gas prices, to stagnating wages, to new technologies enabling a different kind of consumption — has fundamentally changed the game for Millennials. The largest generation in American history might never spend as lavishly as its parents did — nor on the same things. Since the end of World War II, new cars and suburban houses have powered the world's largest economy and propelled our most impressive recoveries. Millennials may have lost interest in both.

11 **What is the main idea of the passage?**

① The direction of responsibility for lower spending levels
② The falling interest in statistical data to describe lifestyles
③ The different spending habits of a new generation
④ The changing consumer bases of core industries

12 **What does the underlined phrase mean?**

① When things are thought to be worse than they are.
② When a good situation is ruined by the incompetence of those in control of it.
③ When environmental factors cause crops to fail, and poverty to rise.
④ When certain things come together at the same moment to make a situation worse.

13 **What can you not infer from the passage?**

① The people controlling the housing and transportation markets have brought this upon themselves.
② Mortgage companies are on the verge of a downturn in business and profits.
③ It is not taken for granted that young people these days will buy a car as soon as possible.
④ Young spenders nowadays are not interested in the things previous generations spent money on.

14-16

Across the country, the teenage pregnancy rate has been declining for decades, a trend experts attribute to improved access to contraceptives as well as to young people delaying having sex longer than they did in the 1990s. There's also less stigma associated with talking frankly and publicly about sex and contraception. From 2005 to 2008, the nation's teen pregnancy rate dropped 37 percent, according to data from the Guttmacher Institute, which works to promote sexual and reproductive health. But progress has been slower in Mississippi, where the teen pregnancy rate fell 20 percent during the same period, the smallest decline of any southern state.

Teen pregnancy in Mississippi is a problem that affects the entire state and cuts across racial and socioeconomic lines, depressing the state's already low graduation rates. Studies have shown more than two-thirds of teenage mothers do not graduate from high school. Moreover, the children of teen parents also graduate at lower rates, and earn less income, than their peers. One report by the Women's Fund estimated that Mississippi taxpayers paid $155 million in 2009 from costs associated with births to teens — costs that included school failure, child neglect, and underemployment.

This fiscal reality helps explain why the culturally conservative state is taking steps to reduce teen pregnancy rates. Virtually overnight, the new law and a grassroots campaign led by a small non-profit called Mississippi First have revamped the way Mississippi schools teach sex education. In the past, most of the state's 151 districts had no formal approach. When the Mississippi Department of Education asked districts for copies of their sex education policies or curricula in 2010, only five had anything written down, according to staff at Mississippi First. At many schools, the entire curriculum consisted of brief seminars with local pastors who preached the sins of pre-marital sex. Others failed to broach the subject at all.

14 Which of the following statements is NOT correct?

① Mississippi is a true representative of the changing rates of teen pregnancy in the US.

② The teenage pregnancy rate in Mississippi is not determined by wealth or race.

③ Sex education in Mississippi pre-2010 was virtually non-existent.

④ Young people are having sex later than they did in the '90s.

15 What was the problem with the previous sex education in Mississippi schools, according to the passage?

① The teachers were unqualified and did not know enough about the subject to teach it properly.

② There were no clear guidelines and information was biased towards abstention rather than choice.

③ The pastors who gave seminars to the schools were often related to the students, making discussion impossible.

④ The school education boards refused to fund the classes, so they were poorly supported.

16 Which of the following is NOT a reason in the passage as to why teenage pregnancy rates are dropping?

① Young people have more access to contraceptives than they ever have before.

② Young people are declining to have sex until much later than before.

③ Sex and contraception are no longer taboo subjects and are discussed more freely than before.

④ The stigma that has been attached to talking about sex and contraception is rising.

17-20

But describing an immigrant as "illegal" is legally inaccurate. Being in the country without proper documents is a civil offense, not a criminal one. (Underscoring this reality, Justice Anthony Kennedy wrote for the majority opinion on SB 1070, Arizona's controversial immigration law: "As a general rule, it is not a crime for a movable alien to remain in the United States.") In a country that believes in due process of the law, calling an immigrant "illegal" is akin to calling a defendant awaiting trial a "criminal." The term "illegal" is also imprecise. For many undocumented people — there are 11 million in the U.S. and most have immediate family members who are American citizens, either by birth or naturalization — their immigration status is fluid and, depending on individual circumstances, can be adjusted.

When journalists, who are supposed to seek neutrality and fairness, use the term, they are politicizing an already political issue. (How can using "illegal immigrant" be considered neutral, for example, when Republican strategist Frank Luntz encouraged using the term in a 2005 memo to tie undocumented people with criminality?) And the term dehumanizes and marginalizes the people it seeks to describe. Think of it this way: (A) If someone is driving a car at 14, we say "underage driver," not "illegal" driver." If someone is driving under the influence, we call them a "drunk driver," not an "illegal driver." Put another way, <u>how would you feel if you — or your family members or friends — were referred to as "illegal"</u>?

17 **What is the topic mainly about?**

① The process whereby an illegal immigrant becomes a US citizen
② The effect of using of the term "illegal immigrant"
③ The correct term that should be used to describe an illegal immigrant
④ The factors that led to the immigration law in Arizona being enacted

18 **What can be inferred from the passage?**

① Frank Luntz wanted people to mentally turn against immigrants.
② Every immigrant in the US is there illegally at first.
③ Justice Anthony Kennedy is a supporter of the controversial Arizona law.
④ Journalists use the term in a political way to prevent any further immigration.

19 **Which of the following sentences best fits the blank (A)?**

① In what other contexts do we call someone illegal?
② Is it polite to label someone as an "illegal" without proof?
③ A criminal is someone who does an act that goes against the determined laws of the state.
④ Those that have been dehumanized and marginalized cannot be described accurately.

20 **Which of the following could replace the underlined phrase?**

① At the point that your friends and family describe you as "illegal", you feel dejected.
② When somebody is labeled as "illegal", we need to be considerate of their friends and family's feelings.
③ It would be terrible if you or those whom you know and love were called "illegal".
④ If you or the people you knew were spoken of as "illegal", would you just take it?

21-23

As travelers, flight delays are something we simply must accept. But those minutes — or hours — of waiting are usually the result of inclement weather, mechanical problems, security scares or even airline glitches. But passengers heading from New York to D.C. earlier this week faced a four-hour delay not for the usual (and, generally, understandable) reasons. Instead, they found themselves waiting because of a tiff between two flight attendants.

American Airlines Flight 3823, set to leave New York's JFK Airport at 3:10 p.m. on Sept. 19, had begun moving along the tarmac, passengers told NBC News, when the fight began. Apparently one flight attendant had been using her cell phone during the crew's pre-departure routine, prompting her co-worker to request that everyone, "including the other flight attendant," needed to turn off all electronic devices.

The comment didn't go over well, and soon, <u>the cockpit crew caught wind of the altercation between the two women</u>. The travelers were then told they'd be returning to the gate "because the flight attendants couldn't work with each other," one passenger told NBC News.

Back at the airport, the passengers had to wait nearly four hours while American Airlines tried finding another flight attendant crew. The original flight had a scheduled gate-to-gate time of one hour and 20 minutes. Travelers described the situation as "ridiculous" and said it was "totally unbelievable that there was such little professionalism." And at a time when it looks like American Airlines is hitting financial turbulence, letting minor tiffs cause major delays just isn't going to fly.

21 **What can be inferred from the passage?**

① The two flight attendants threatened to cause an in-air incident if not allowed to disembark the plane.

② These kind of personal arguments happen often to flight attendants.

③ American Airlines customers can expect further delays in the near future.

④ The situation will not have helped American Airlines' image or stabilized its future.

22 **What started the argument, according to the passage?**

① One flight attendant embarrassed another by reminding her, publicly in front of the passengers, not to use her cell phone.

② One flight attendant was annoyed that she was not able to use her cell phone, but another had been allowed to do so.

③ One flight attendant resented the fact that cell phones were banned for flight attendants, in addition to passengers.

④ One flight attendant was distracted and not paying enough attention to the more senior flight attendant.

23 **How can the underlined phrase be restated?**

① the pilot and co-pilot heard about the two women's quarrel.

② those flying the airplane tried to ignore the two women's argument.

③ the people in the cockpit were not initially informed of the situation.

④ the entire crew was told of the fight and asked for their help.

24-27

Brazil, Russia, India, China and South Africa recently concluded the fifth annual meeting of the countries known collectively as the BRICs. Or should that be the BRICS? The confusion arises from the fact that South Africa has sneaked into the group, which claims to represent the world's emerging markets and act as a counterweight to the G8 and G20, which are dominated by rich-world economies. The BRIC countries were the constituent members of an acronym coined by Jim O'Neill, then of Goldman Sachs, in 2001. Mr O'Neill was looking for a way to convey the fact that much of the world's economic growth would soon come from Brazil, Russia, India and China. There was much debate about whether this grouping made sense: at the time Brazil's growth seemed too sluggish to warrant inclusion; now Russia looks like it doesn't deserve to be placed with the others. China has a much higher economic growth rate than the rest. Even so, the label proved so catchy that the foreign ministers of the BRIC countries decided to hold a summit in New York in 2006. What began as a hook for an investment bank's research note became a real political institution.

There was just one problem with the BRICs: no African countries were included. This was a little embarrassing. Overlooking Africa suggested that the continent was an economic irrelevance, good only for providing raw materials to the rest. <u>It also cast doubt on the group's claim to speak for the emerging world</u>. Two African countries might have been candidates, Nigeria and South Africa. But only one would keep the acronym intact. And so, in 2010, the club of BRICs became the BRICS. The strange etymology of the BRICS has real-world consequences. Though the inter-governmental meetings have not amounted to much yet, these countries do have ambitions to set up a joint investment bank.

24 What do the members of BRICS have in common?

① All the members had felt unfairly excluded from the G8 and G20 meetings of the richer economies.
② At the time that the term was coined, they were considered the strongest emerging economies.
③ They had at one time been a member of the rich economies but had fallen on hard times.
④ They had previously claimed that each represented their continent financially.

25 What was the purpose of Mr O'Neill's coining of the term?

① To placate countries with which Goldman Sachs wished to conduct business
② To demonstrate the ineffectiveness of creating acronyms in economy
③ To distinguish between existing strong economies and emerging ones
④ To indicate where the world's future strong economies lay

26 What cannot be inferred from the passage?

① South Africa had no economic right to be included in BRIC.
② Nigeria's name was not considered the right fit for BRIC.
③ So far BRIC has had little impact on the global financial stage.
④ The creation of BRIC was not wholly accurate as the members are not equal today.

27 Which of the following correctly resembles the underlined?

① It contradicted the claim that they were symbols of the emerging world.
② It made the emerging world doubt whether it had been protected.
③ It led to claims that they were only after benefits for themselves.
④ Other emerging world nations claimed that the group did not speak for them.

28-30

Smoking at once relaxes and stimulates the body. Seconds after inhalation nicotine reaches the brain and binds to receptor molecules on nerve cells, triggering the cells to release a flood of dopamine and other neurotransmitters that washes over pleasure centers. A few more puffs increase heart rate, raising alertness. The effect does not last long, however, spurring smokers to light up again. Over time the number of nicotinic receptors increases — and the need to smoke again to reduce withdrawal symptoms such as irritability. ______________________, smoking becomes linked with everyday behavior or moods: drinking coffee or a bout of boredom, for instance, might also trigger the desire to reach for a cigarette — all making it difficult to kick the habit.

28 Which of the following is NOT an effect of smoking?

① Having a bad temper when one is not able to smoke freely.
② Causing the smoker to feel more tranquil than they were before they lit up.
③ Prompts the smoker to make more friends and meet new people.
④ Using cigarettes as a solution to relieving other behavioral problems.

29 Which of the following can be inferred from the passage?

① As soon as you have started smoking, your yearning to smoke will never leave you.
② Dopamine is connected to the body feeling pleasure.
③ Somebody who smokes a lot is liable to suffer from heart disease.
④ From the very first puff, a smoker feels at ease with the act of smoking.

30 Choose the one that best fills in the blank.

① On the contrary ② As a result of this
③ On top of that ④ In addition to

20 Practice Test

Read the following passages and answer the questions. [01~30] (제한 시간: 45분)

Of all intervention methods, price has been shown to be the single most effective means of reducing tobacco use. However, a common argument raised against increased tobacco excise taxes is that such increased tax rates will lead to either illegal smuggling of cigarettes across state borders, or that they will lead to decreased revenue for the state because smokers will find other sources for cheaper cigarettes, via the Internet or across state borders. This has not proven to be the case in states that have raised taxes. Research has shown that behavior such as tax avoidance and smuggling are not common.

01 **What is the main idea of this passage?**

① The unfairness of excise tax on a tobacco company.

② That taxes on cigarettes can in fact be raised without much worry.

③ The results of placing too much tax on a product.

④ What people want to be done about the excise taxes on tobacco products.

02-03

The young Emperor Nero became known as one of the worst Roman rulers by ordering his mother's death, persecuting Christians and Jews and committing other cruel and bizarre deeds. And, of course, it has also been suggested that he even gave a musical recital, with himself as sole performer, while Rome was ablaze with a fire he had caused. Nero's behavior has come under fresh scholarly discussion, nourished by recent study of ancient Roman chronicles, sculpture, ruins and coins. Though he is still seen as profoundly ruthless, new research makes him seem more understandable by emphasizing that his reign was shaped by his serious passion for the arts, among other personal traits, and by complicated political problems.

02 **Why has the traditional opinion on Nero come under scrutiny?**

① Many other traditional hate figures of classical history have seen their personalities rewritten by modern scholars, so scholars wanted to see if they could also do so with Nero.

② Much of Nero's life was unknown and was guessed about but has since been cemented as being true.

③ Scholars are tired of churning out the same material again and again and they want to inject life into his image.

④ Evidence has come to light that seems to paint a different picture of his personality and the time in which he lived.

03 **Which of the following is not one of Nero's evil deeds?**

① He requested that his mother be murdered.

② He did not care that Rome was burning.

③ He harassed Christians and Jews.

④ He ordered the murder of all artists.

04–05

Shall we read them in the first place to satisfy that curiosity which possesses us sometimes when in the evening we linger in front of a house where the lights are lit and the blinds not yet drawn, and each floor of the house shows us a different section of human life in being? Then we are consumed with curiosity about the lives of these people — the servants gossiping, the gentlemen dining, the girl dressing for a party, the old woman at the window with her knitting. Who are they, what are they, what are their names, their occupations, their thoughts, and adventures? Biographies and memoirs answer such questions, light up innumerable such houses; they show us people going about their daily affairs, toiling, failing, succeeding, eating, hating, loving, until they die. And sometimes as we watch, the house fades and the iron railings vanish and we are out at sea; we are hunting, sailing, fighting; we are among savages and soldiers; we are taking part in great campaigns.

04 **What do biographies do, according to the passage?**

① They teach us a better way to live our lives and how to get the most out of it.
② They show us how good life could be if we were in another person's shoes.
③ They give us a glimpse into another person's life and take us on their own personal journey.
④ They expose all the negative points of the human psyche that should remain hidden.

05 **What can be inferred from the passage?**

① It takes a certain kind of person to be fascinated by biographies of random people.
② The best biographies are those about people who have done great things and achieved elevated heights.
③ When reading biographies, we need to make sure that we give the subjects our respect.
④ People who enjoy reading biographies are curious about human nature and others' lives.

06-08

Helping their children learn remotely during the pandemic has driven many parents to distraction. A few have found it easier and more rewarding to take complete control of their children's lessons. Research published in November by the Association of Directors of Children's Services, a group that represents local officials, found the number of home-educated children in England had increased by 40% to about 75,000 in the year to October 2020. [A] That represents a little under 1% of school-aged children but it is double the number who were home educated four years before. In America, where some schools have not opened their buildings since March, the numbers are higher. [B] A survey published in October by the Pew Research Center found that around 7% of American parents were formally home-schooling their children, up from around 3% in the spring. The ranks of home educators were swelling long before the disruption of covid-19. [C] But since 2007 the share of parents who say that providing religious or moral instruction is the "most important" reason for them to home-school has fallen, according to a survey by the Department of Education. [D] More parents now cite concerns about drugs and other nasty influences in schools. Those who live near bad schools and who cannot afford private ones sometimes decide home-schooling is a better option. Black families and those from other minorities have additional worries about racism in the public school system, too.

06 **What is the main idea of the passage?**

① The number of home-educated children has risen because of the pandemic but it had already been increasing.

② Parents don't want to home-educate their children, but the pandemic forced them to take do it.

③ The attitude towards home education of children has changed from negative to positive in the US and the UK.

④ Home education was frowned up on before the pandemic but now it is looked favorably upon.

07 **Why might parents decide to home-educate their children, according to the passage?**

① They want their children to focus on study in stead of making friends and playing.

② They want to shield their children from bad influences in the school environment.

③ They believe that they are better teachers than those in charge of their children.

④ They do not want their children to become sick from interaction with other children.

08 **Which is the best place for the following passage?**

For decades the greatest number in America have been conservative Christians who fear public schools may corrupt their offspring.

① [A]　　② [B]

③ [C]　　④ [D]

09-11

Some striking evidence is available in the research of psychologist Robert O'Connor on socially withdrawn preschool children. We have all seen children of this sort, terribly shy, standing alone at the fringes of the games and groupings of their peers. O'Connor worried that a long-term pattern of isolation was forming, even at an early age, that would create persistent difficulties in social comfort and adjustment through adulthood. In an attempt to reverse the pattern, O'Connor made a film containing eleven different scenes in a nursery-school setting. Each scene began by showing a different solitary child watching some ongoing social activity and then actively joining the activity, to everyone's enjoyment. O'Connor selected a group of the most severely withdrawn children from four preschools and showed them his film. The impact was impressive. The isolates immediately began to interact with their peers at a level equal to that of the normal children in the schools.

Even more astonishing was what O'Connor found when he returned to observe six weeks later. While the withdrawn children who had not seen O'Connor's film remained as isolated as ever, those who had viewed it were now leading their schools in amount of social activity. It seems that this twenty-three minute movie, viewed just once, was enough to reverse a potential pattern of lifelong maladaptive behavior.

09 **What is the idea of the passage?**

① There are numerous unknown effects of changing the social interaction of children.

② The likely reasons for children to be socially awkward lie in their friendships.

③ It is possible to alter the character of socially withdrawn children.

④ Identifying the problems in withdrawn children is easier than solving them.

10 **What can be inferred about the withdrawn children?**

① It took enormous courage for them to step into a circle of socially comfortable children.

② After the withdrawn child joined the activity, the group's ambience began to change.

③ After seeing other children like themselves begin to interact, they realized they could do the same.

④ The withdrawn children who saw the film thought that they were witnessing their own transformation.

11 **What was in the film?**

① The interaction of socially awkward children and normal children as they learn to treat one other better.

② The behavior of socially withdrawn children before and after being treated psychologically.

③ A large group of children who each find it hard to be socially comfortable learn to befriend one another.

④ A series of children who ordinarily retreat from group interaction joining in and having fun.

12-14

“Lifestyle” is an example of terminology that was adopted by consumers even before the marketing community. “Lifestyle,” like “imagine” and the “American Dream,” is incredibly powerful because it is at the same time self-defined and aspirational — everyone defines and aspires to his or her own unique lifestyle. But unlike the “American Dream,” the concept of “lifestyle” is a relatively new term. The compound word was created in 1929 by Alfred Adler, an Austrian scientist, but today’s definition of the word wasn’t applied until the 1960s. The word “lifestyle” both creates and exemplifies a Weltanschauung or world-view (speaking of German-derived compound words) — one that is individualistic rather than community-oriented, personalized rather than generic, and forward-looking rather than nostalgic or tethered to tradition. The very notion of styling one’s life — and that there are many different styles of the good life from which to choose — would have seemed a foreign and bizarre concept to our great-grandparents. Yet “lifestyle” is a concept that is essential to understanding our more secular, individualist age.
“Lifestyle” implies that there is more than one model of “the good life,” and all we have to do is choose. This may be relativistic or self-centered, but we live in an era of individuality, and choosing a lifestyle is a crucial component of defining who we are. Today, “lifestyle” has special currency among young people, who use it to describe what they like, what they believe, and what they want to do. It’s a catch-all term. Instead of talking about how they eat, what they do for exercise, or how much they work, they talk about their “lifestyle” as a whole. All the various facets, instead of being examined individually, are subsumed into the larger “lifestyle” context. It’s no longer a question of what I want for a career or where I want to live or what I do for fun — that’s just a subset of the larger question: What lifestyle do I want to make for myself?

12 **What is the topic of the passage?**

① The meaning of lifestyle to today's generation.
② The difference between lifestyle and the American Dream.
③ The implications of choosing your own lifestyle.
④ The individualism of the lifestyle of modern society.

13 **Which of the following is true about lifestyle?**

① Lifestyle was unknown in America until Alfred Adler introduced it.
② People aspire to have their own personal lifestyle that gives them pleasure.
③ Having a unique lifestyle implies a more introspective outlook on life.
④ Previous generations adhered to different lifestyles but equally individualistic.

14 **What does the underlined mean?**

① It's a word that covers a wide range of meanings.
② It's a word that is used by many different kinds of people.
③ It's a word that can be grasped by people from all walks of life.
④ It's a word that denotes specific things to specific people.

15-17

Without fictions we would be less aware of the importance of freedom for life to be livable, the hell it turns into when it is trampled underfoot by a tyrant, an ideology, or a religion. Let those who doubt that literature not only submerges us in the dream of beauty and happiness but alerts us to every kind of oppression, ask themselves why all regimes determined to control the behavior of citizens ______________________ fear it so much they establish systems of censorship to repress it and keep so wary an eye on independent writers. They do this because they know the risk of allowing the imagination to wander free in books, know how seditious fictions become when the reader compares the freedom that makes them possible and is exercised in them with the obscurantism and fear lying in wait in the real world. Whether they want it or not, know it or not, when they invent stories the writers of tales propagate dissatisfaction, demonstrating that the world is badly made and the life of fantasy richer than the life of our daily routine. This fact, if it takes root in their sensibility and consciousness, makes citizens more difficult to manipulate, less willing to accept the lies of the interrogators and jailers who would like to make them believe that behind bars they lead more secure and better lives.

15 **What is the main idea of the passage?**

① Fictions open our eyes to the fact that the real world is lacking in something.
② Writers are needed in society because without them we would feel nothing.
③ Fictions have long been subjected to censorship because they are written by intelligent people.
④ People who do not read fictions are more likely to accept others unconditionally.

16 **What can you infer from the passage?**

① Those who are dissatisfied with life do not need to read fictions in order to know what is wrong.
② Governments that do not censor literature leave themselves open to criticism.
③ Fictions teach us to fear those who are above us and what they may do to us.
④ People who read are naturally more argumentative than those who do not.

17 **Which of the following phrases fits the blank?**

① from cradle to grave
② from their home to wherever they go
③ through the Internet
④ through the creation and mediation of online communities

18-20

[A] In fact this is an old idea dressed up to look new. Some Jews argued for a single binational state in the Holy Land long before Israel was created. Today, for those in Israel and abroad who find the idea of a state where everybody has to share ethnicity or religion antiquated, a single state sounds enticing. Those Israelis who abhor the idea of giving up any territory to the Palestinians, meanwhile, like the idea because it sounds as though they get to hold on to what they have. And to some outsiders, the one-state solution is appealing because the negotiation that might lead to separate states is so hard and has made so little progress.

[B] One goal of American foreign policy is the creation of a separate Palestinian state alongside Israel—the famed two-state solution to peace in the Middle East. Lately, however, there has been much talk of a one-state solution to this intractable problem. What's going on?

[C] At some point in the future, demography will force Israel to choose between being a predominantly Jewish state or being a democracy, because Palestinians within Israel are reproducing at a faster rate than Israeli Jews. The only way to avoid this choice is to create a separate, viable state for Palestinians. Which suggests that people will revert to talking about a two-state solution before long.

[D] People who talk of a one-state solution can thus mean completely different and incompatible things. On the hard right of Israeli politics it means expelling Palestinians to some third country (Jordan is frequently mentioned, though the Jordanians have no interest in this). For those on the left who favour a single state, it means a multi-ethnic, multi-confessional country in which a Palestinian Muslim might one day become prime minister. These two sides are not about to agree.

18 **Choose the most logical order of the following paragraphs.**

① [B] – [C] – [A] – [D]
② [C] – [D] – [B] – [A]
③ [C] – [B] – [A] – [D]
④ [B] – [A] – [D] – [C]

19 **What is the conclusion of the passage?**

① The popular debate of the one-state solution means that people will realize how difficult it would be to implement, so the two-state solution will soon be on the table again.
② Israel will follow a two-state solution because it so fears the one-state solution that it is not prepared to concede any ground to the Palestinians.
③ Neither party wants to be responsible for making the final choice for a one-state solution; therefore, a two-state solution is preferred.
④ Palestinians will soon outnumber Israeli Jews, so a two-state solution is being considered to preserve territory for the Israeli Jews.

20 **How do the left and right wing differ in how they see the one-state solution?**

① The right wing does not trust the Palestinians to keep their promise while the left wing thinks that the Israeli Jews are liars.
② A one-state solution would be acceptable to both right and left wing if the leaders could get along and make a show of solidarity.
③ The left wing views the right as looking for a traditional solution while the right wing sees only naive youth on the left wing.
④ Right wing people want to expel the Palestinians from Israel while left wing people want them all to live peacefully side by side.

21-24

When I was a child, my mother used to tell me, "It's not what you say, it's how you say it." Years later, I find myself saying the same thing to my own kids. Their behavior reminds me daily how much of our attitude is revealed not by words but by the way they are spoken.

Two dialogues really take place in every conversation — one uses words, the other tone of voice. Sometimes the two match, but often they do not. When you ask someone, "How are you?" and get the reply "Fine," you're not usually relying on the word "fine" to tell you how she feels. Instead, you let her tone tell you whether she really is fine, or whether she is depressed, anxious, excited, or feeling any of a dozen other emotions. When you listen to tone, volume, cadence, and other vocal characteristics, you tune in to the nonverbal conversation, where the true substance is often found.

Anyone with normal hearing can detect the signals people convey with their tone of voice, but few of us understand all of them. This is partly because when we're interacting with someone, there's a lot of competition for our attention. We size up their appearance and body language, listen to the content of their words, and watch their actions. We may even struggle to identify some intuitive reaction we're having to the person or situation. Vocal subtleties can get lost in all this. It's easy to notice the message someone sends with a pouty, sad, or frustrated tone of voice, but a fleeting note of anxiety, fear, or embarrassment may slip right past you if you don't pay close attention.

21 **Which of the following is not mentioned as something you should focus on when someone speaks?**

① How loudly the person is speaking.
② The attitude that is conveyed when the person is speaking.
③ The rhythm of the words that the person is using.
④ The particular words the person has chosen to express a feeling.

22 How do we know if someone feels fine?

① We listen to the way someone says the word, rather than just concentrating on the meaning of the word "fine".

② We look closely at what has happened to the person up to the point that he or she says that they feel fine.

③ We should get to know the person's life so that we can determine their mood patterns and know what they truly mean when he or she says fine.

④ We have to ask the person to elaborate on their answer instead of just accepting what they say first.

23 What can be inferred from the passage?

① The things that are left unsaid in conversations are often the most important parts.

② Most people do not pick up on various things that are going on during conversations.

③ The first thing anyone should do in a conversation is to size up the other person physically.

④ It's not difficult to pick up all the signals in a conversation with a little bit of focus.

24 Which of the following correctly paraphrases the underlined?

① The dialogue and the tone of voice that you use can mean the difference between two conversations.

② In order to ensure each conversation is different, you need to pay attention to dialogue and tone of voice.

③ When you examine two dialogues, you notice that words and tone of voice change meanings.

④ When we speak, we partake in two conversations of dialogue and tone of voice.

25–28

Listen carefully to what others say about you, whether they're delivering the message in apparent jest or with utmost sincerity. If people comment on your appearance or occasionally mention one of your mannerisms, ask yourself why. Don't casually dismiss what may have been efforts to politely tip you off to your offensive habits. As my mother used to say, "Never turn down a mint. You never know why it's being offered." And don't ignore others' comments just because they're made casually or in jest. When someone says, "Just kidding," they probably aren't.

This point was brought home early on in jury selection for the O. J. Simpson trial, when Marcia Clark asked a juror if she had said or done anything to offend her. The juror, a conservative, older Italian-American woman, responded, "Well, your skirts are too short."

Given the juror's age and cultural background, this objection wasn't surprising, but it was a small shock to hear it spoken so directly. Some people in the courtroom suppressed a giggle or two, and in general the comment wasn't taken very seriously at the time. I thought about that juror later, however, when the media seemed obsessed with the length of Ms. Clark's skirts. Apparently, that elderly woman's opinion wasn't so far off the mark after all.

25 **What is the passage mainly about?**

① Being polite to those who have not made the effort to be polite to you.

② Listening and taking on board what someone has to say.

③ Reading the language of others who do not like you.

④ Responding to criticism well.

26 What does the story about the juror tell us?

① Lawyers should not try to directly interact with jurors who they think may not give them a warm response.

② Jurors have prejudices that cannot be brushed under the carpet and should be taken into account in jury selection.

③ Direct responses are sometimes not taken seriously, but they may be closer to the truth than you think.

④ Asking someone a direct question can sometimes elicit a response that you may not want to hear.

27 What does the underlined saying mean?

① You could be offered a mint because you have bad breath rather than just as a courtesy.

② Mints are offered for a variety of reasons and you can never guess which one is being thought of.

③ By turning down mints you may be offending the person who offered them.

④ Somebody may be offering you a mint out of kindness, so don't take it to heart.

28 Which of the following can be inferred?

① If you have some bad habits, remember to suppress them and listen to other people's advice.

② People who try to point out your bad habits are doing so just to be mean, so ignore them.

③ Somebody might be trying to casually point out your bad habit, so listen carefully.

④ Ask a friend to be honest in her opinion of your bad habits in order to eliminate them.

29–30

There is little downside when men negotiate for themselves. People expect men to advocate on their own behalf, point out their contributions, and be recognized and rewarded for them. For men, there is truly no harm in asking. But since women are expected to be concerned with others, when they advocate for themselves or point to their own value, both men and women react unfavorably. Interestingly, women can negotiate as well as or even more successfully than men when negotiating for others (such as their company or a colleague), because in these cases, their advocacy does not make them appear self-serving. However, when a woman negotiates on her own behalf, she violates the perceived gender norm. Both male and female colleagues often resist working with a woman who has negotiated for a higher salary because she's seen as more demanding than a woman who refrained from negotiating. Even when a woman negotiates successfully for herself, she can pay a longer-term cost in goodwill and future advancement. Regrettably, all women are Heidi. Try as we might, we just can't be Howard.

29 **What is the idea of the passage?**

① A woman needs to act like a man to be taken seriously in the workplace, but she has to do it subtly.

② Women's negotiating skills are not comparable to the superior ability of men doing the same thing.

③ A woman who does something in her own interest appears self-serving and is thought of negatively.

④ When a woman decides to do something purely for herself, she has to be careful not to flaunt it.

30 **What does the underlined mean?**

① Women will never be thought of in the same way as men because they can't change their gender.

② Women are women and men are men even though some people have made the switch successfully.

③ Women are expected to have both male and female traits when they are just women.

④ Women keep trying to be equal to men but most of them fail miserably.

홍준기 교수

주요 약력

現. 박문각편입학원 총괄 디렉터 겸 대표 교수
Korea JoongAng Daily 객원 해설위원
Korea JoongAng Daily 독해 연재 매주(토요일) (2013. 1. ~ 현재)
前. 시설관리공단 공채 시험 영어과 출제 위원
KBS 굿모닝팝스 독해 연재

주요 저서

- 박문각 편입 문법 시리즈 (박문각출판 刊)
- 박문각 편입 독해 시리즈 (박문각출판 刊)
- 박문각 편입 논리 시리즈 (박문각출판 刊)
- 박문각 편입 어휘 시리즈 (박문각출판 刊)
- 박문각 편입 적중 모의고사 (박문각출판 刊)
- 공무원 VOCA 마스터 (박문각출판 刊)
- 석세스 편입독해/편입논리 (종합출판Eng 刊)
- 스타영문법사전(공저) (종로편입아카데미 刊)
- 영문법 Restart(공저) (종합출판Eng 刊)
- 중앙데일리 리딩 스펙트럼(Ⅰ – Ⅳ) (종합출판Eng 刊)
- 시사독해 실렉션 (종합출판Eng 刊)

동영상 강의
www.pmg.co.kr

박문각 편입
실전 독해

초판 인쇄 2021년 7월 1일 | **초판 발행** 2021년 7월 5일
편저 홍준기 | **발행인** 박 용 | **발행처** (주)박문각출판
등록 2015년 4월 29일 제2015-000104호
주소 06654 서울시 서초구 효령로 283 서경 B/D 4층
팩스 (02)584-2927 | **전화** 교재 주문 (02)6466-7202

저자와의 협의하에 인지생략

정가 28,000원(정답 및 해설 포함)
ISBN 979-11-6704-119-7
ISBN 979-11-6704-118-0(세트)